WORK FROM HOME

CONTENTS

ACKNOWLEDGEMENTS 7

INTRODUCTION 8

Part 1 10

Sounds like a Nice Idea 10

Chapter 1 11

WHY DO YOU WORK FROM HOME? 11

WHY DO YOU WORK FROM HOME? 12

Who is Eligible to Work Remotely? 17

What makes working from home so beneficial? 18

Negative Effects of Working from Home 22

Is Working from home for me? 25

Chapter 2 26

CAN I WORK FROM HOME AND BE SUCCESSFUL? 26

Why Character Matters 27

Why Different People Have Different Perspectives 35

WHY DO YOU GET OUT OF BED IN THE MORNING? 40

Decision After Decision 44

Chapter 3 46

AM I ABLE TO WORK FROM HOME? 46

"Opportunity" for doing homework. 46

Is working remotely for a company the appropriate move? 47

How to convince your employer to let you work from home.................51

As your own boss, you can earn money from home. 53

Understanding the complexities of self-employment paperwork 61

Taking care of your finances as a self-employed person..................67

People you should be aware of while starting a business..................72

Part 2 77

Making it Happen..................77

4 78

HOW DO I CREATE MY PERFECT WORKSPACE? 78

Organizing or upgrading your workspace 78

Should I open my office to visitors? 93

A Substitute for Home Meetings..................95

5 99

CAN I BE PRODUCTIVE AT HOME?..................99

Are you productive or sluggish, miserable, and fat? 100

Identifying your most effective working from home habits..................101

Establishing A Daily Schedule and Maintaining Concentration 105

BEING EFFICIENT WITH YOUR TIME 110

ELIMINATING TIME WASTERS 112

HOW TO STOP PROCRASTINATING AND WHAT YOU CAN DO..................117

6 122

WHAT ABOUT MY PROFESSIONAL IMAGE?..................122

The significance of confidentiality..................123

DELIVERING TOP-NOTCH CLIENT SERVICE 124

Having the appropriate appearance and Behaviour..................129

Keeping up with the times while working..................138

Self-employed should have consistent branding 141

PART 3 147

SECRETS OF SUCCESS 147

7 148

WON'T I FEEL ISOLATED? 148

Managing Isolation 149

GOING OUTSIDE MORE 151

WHY ARE PEOPLE NETWORKING? 154

WEB-BASED NETWORKING 161

8 164

HOW DO I KEEP HOME AND WORK SEPARATED? 164

While working from home, you should take care of yourself 165

TAKING CARE OF FAMILY AND FRIENDS 174

MAINTAINING YOUR PRIMARY RELATIONSHIP...............176

PROVIDING AND OBTAINING FEEDBACK 178

WORKING FROM HOME AND CHILDREN...........................184

HAVING TEENAGERS AND WORKING FROM HOME 186

MANAGING VISITORS IN YOUR HOME..............................187

9 189

IF A CRISIS ARISES, WHAT THEN?....................................189

WHAT MIGHT POSSIBLY FAIL? 189

EMERGENCIES INVOLVING FAMILY AND THE HOME 192

Individual Issues 194

UNFAVORABLE CIRCUMSTANCES....................................195

GETTING HUNG UP...195

TIME IS OF THE ESSENCE 195

A WONDERFUL CHANCE 196

HOW TO STAY CALM DURING TIMES OF CRISIS 196

REMOVE YOURSELF FROM THE ISSUE. 197

BELIEVE IN YOUR INSTINCTS 197

ACT IN A DIFFERENT WAY..197

Plan Ahead...200

Choose Your Answer. 204

Don't enquire as to why, but do request feedback 205

You "can't win them all," 206

Failures Happen to Even the Most Successful Persons 206

Failure Does Not Exist; Feedback Does..207

Share Your Pain 207

Simply Move Forward. 207

Recognize the Situation...208

Laughing is Necessary. 209

AFTERWORD..210

ACKNOWLEDGEMENTS

I would like to thank the following people for their assistance in making this book possible: Thanks to Anthonia for all the encouragement and emotional support. I cannot forget to mention Jephrrey Mohantin who was consistent with educational contents, to ensure this book comes to reality.

I haven't been able to mention my employer: Robinson Dwart, who gave me the opportunity to experience the joy of working from home during the Covid-19 pandemic, this was the starting point of my being enlightened of the freedom of working from home.

My sincere appreciation goes to everyone who has contributed in one way or the other to the success of this book. Special thanks go to Geeth Mohit, who provided me with important instructions through content creation, regular feedback, and shared his time and experience with me. I appreciate you all and say a big thank you.

INTRODUCTION

Do you belong to the countless numbers of people who have already discovered the advantages of working from home? Or perhaps you're one of those people debating making the leap but unsure of what obstacles you'll encounter? If so, this book just could be the one to do it. As someone who has nearly 20 years of experience working from home, I am well aware of all the benefits and drawbacks. To start making money, all I had to do was sit down at my desk and pull out my timesheet.

I am free to plan my day how I choose. I can set an early alarm if I have a deadline.
and begin working right away. Perhaps I could finish up the dishes from last night or the laundry prior to turning on my computer. If I lose motivation or interest during the day, I take a stroll, nap, or leave to run errands. At times, I just don't start to pick up until dusk, after which I can continue working until I'm prepared to go to sleep.

Working from home is unquestionably the finest method for life organization. It provides flexibility and control, saves time, and uses less fuel, extra time to spend with friends and family. You therefore have a long way to go. When all of your activities are concentrated in one place, you live more comfortably instead of two or perhaps more.

The number of people in the UK who work from home is currently projected to be over 3 million, and in the next years, it is anticipated to increase significantly. Because of this, I made the decision to create a working from home manual that both employees and independent contractors may use. Not who pays your money, but where you earn it, is the deciding issue in this situation. Work is what you do, not where you go, as I once read. No matter if you own your own business or work for a major corporation, you will share experiences and seek out answers to related problems.

You don't have to read the entire book from cover to cover; instead, start with the sections that are now the most important to you and then dip in and out as you have the time and need. If you're pressed for time, each chapter begins with a synopsis of the key ideas, followed by a list of helpful resources, so you can start making changes right away.

I sincerely hope you appreciate this book and find it useful in maximizing your benefits from working from home.

Part 1

Sounds like a Nice Idea

Chapter 1

WHY DO YOU WORK FROM HOME?

Just a few years ago, leaving for work every morning was the norm, and anyone who worked from home was the exception. Yes, times have changed.

changed. There are now three times as many people working from home as there were in 1997, when the Office for National Statistics began collecting statistics on the topic. According to the Labour Market Trends survey from 2005, 3.1 million people—or 11% of the workforce in the UK—worked from home full-time, and many more did so sometimes. And it would appear that many office workers have this as their goal.

"According to a 2007 survey by the insurance business Cornhill Direct, 69% of workers said they would want to work from home if given the option. One in five people stated they were so eager to do it that they would take a pay cut."

WorkWise UK, a company that promotes smarter working methods, forecasted that by 2012, an astounding 50% of the workforce would be working from home.

Given your situation, you may have thought about doing your own homework but decided against it. But a variety of people succeed in working from home for a variety of reasons, which may improve their lives. This chapter will go over the reasons why so many people have already chosen to work from home instead of going to the office in order to help you evaluate the facts of your own situation.

The following topics are covered in this chapter:

1. The causes for the more than 3 million people who already work from home and the projected fast increase in that number.
2. How you, whether you are self-employed or employed by another person, can work from home.
3. Benefits to you, your company, the community, and the environment from working remotely.
4. Before making a decision, carefully evaluate the drawbacks of working from home.
5. A questionnaire to assess your level of readiness to start working from home and what information will best prepare you for it.

WHY DO YOU WORK FROM HOME?

When we consider the several variables - economic, social, and political - that are causing fewer individuals to commute daily to a central location, we can conclude that there are over three million British homemakers and growing. The rise in numbers is not surprising. Each person who does their homework does so for a variety of different reasons. The need to reduce transportation costs at a time when housing and utility costs are eating up more discretionary income than ever before is only one of them. Others include the desire to live a less stressed life and spend more time with their family. Concerns about pollution and climate change are also driving the increase in remote work because so many more occupations can now be done that way.

APPLY THE USE OF TECHNOLOGY

We can now transfer information at a scale and speed that have never been possible before thanks to the internet. Huge files that formerly required physical delivery can now be sent and received thanks to the development of broadband. People can now complete a variety of tasks at home without having to leave their homes to visit a library or the corporate office to get professional information. We can find professionals wherever we are; thanks to sophisticated search engines. With video-conferencing, multinational corporations may hold international meetings without flying anyone anywhere. Before meeting with clients, salespeople check the company intranet for the most recent prices and stock levels, and they submit orders online right away. Mobile phones enable us to communicate with co-workers around the world around-the-clock. With a great website, you may run your own business without anyone knowing or even caring where you are located. You're using a computer, yet there are issues? Remote access enables IT personnel to examine the issue and make a fix while apart. Additionally, you may remotely backup all of that important data when you want to ensure that it meets with legal standards, is protected from fire, flood, or theft.

HAVE A BETTER BALANCE BETWEEN YOUR LIFE AND YOUR JOB

The amount of time employees waste traveling to and from work and during their free time is becoming old. Instead of being at their offices or with their families, they are standing in lines and crammed into trains. People who can make a living distant from the major commercial hubs are relocating as daily commuting is taxing, stressful, and expensive. You have control over every part of your life when you work from home, so you don't have to follow office culture and can do your work whenever you choose. Nobody will be staring at you if you ignore the phone ringing while you're focused. The jigsaw puzzle pieces can all be put together anyway is most practical for you. If I hadn't been working from home for the past five years, I have no idea how I could have managed my life satisfactorily. I've experienced a variety of commitments across the UK, sometimes at short notice, but somehow, with the freedom I have in my working life, it all works out and everything gets done.

AVOID SPENDING MONEY

It's undeniable that today's commute costs outrageous amounts of money. If you own a car, you must pay for gas, parking, and maybe road tolls and the congestion charge depending on where you live. Additionally, you must not even consider going over the allotted time on your parking ticket or stopping on a double yellow line to buy a pint of milk on the way home. You have to deal with rising costs for services that are getting more and more congested, delays, and unforeseen cancellations if you take public transportation.

It costs money just to be an employee. Going along for the coffees, lunches, and drinks after work—and possibly some dinners and evenings out as well—allows you to blend in and avoid being perceived as odd or standoffish. As the well-groomed professional by day and the stylish partygoer by night, you must also dress the role. To avoid being the depressing person who always wears the same thing, you should have a sufficient amount of clothes to mix and match. Additionally, have you ever observed that suits and "business clothes" require dry cleaning almost every time they are worn?

You probably already know if you have kids or plan to have kids in the near future that the price of day care has been steadily rising over the past few years, rising at a rate far higher than the rate of inflation.

Parents are growing hesitant to pay nursery fees when you consider this coupled with the current, well reported concerns about the quality of care and security at nurseries. How much more advantageous would it be to juggle your work to fit around naptimes, playdates, and bedtimes?

All of us are well aware of the exorbitant costs associated with purchasing or leasing real estate, including commercial property. According to BT, each employee who works from home annually saves the company an average of £6,000 on office expenses. Additionally, if you were self-employed, it's likely that you wouldn't still be operating. If the cost of purchasing or leasing commercial property is included, many business strategies simply fall short. If we had to operate our cleaning service from a commercial space, it never would have taken off, and even when it started to turn a profit, I never thought about taking it out of the house.

AID IN RESISTING CLIMATE CHANGE

When food was transported by air from areas like South America and Africa to British supermarkets, there was a great deal of worry about the "food miles" involved. Since then, there has been a discernible increase in the popularity of farmers' markets and a significant focus on promoting regional and seasonal foods.

But have you heard of "work miles," or the lengths that commuters log every day as they go to and from their jobs? If not, you might not have to wait too long. In a world of traffic, pollution, and expensive gas, it makes less and less sense for thousands of individuals to spend hours each working day commuting to and from a place of employment when they can complete the same tasks more efficiently at home.

Since unexpected and extreme weather events now frequently occur in the UK, such as the heavy rain that caused the summer floods of 2007, there is more public discussion about the implications of climate change and how reducing carbon emissions from driving could help to halt or reverse the effects.

Individual carbon permits or carbon credit cards were first suggested by David Miliband, who was the secretary of state for environment, food, and rural affairs at the time. Customers would need to carry a swipe card that tracks their carbon limit, and points would be subtracted each time they refilled their gas tank or purchased a plane ticket. Unused points could be sold to a central bank by those who have them.

REDUCE USE OF OIL SUPPLIES

Since the availability of cheap oil and continuous economic expansion served as the cornerstones of the western world, the concept of "peak oil," or the point at which global oil supplies can no longer keep up with demand and begin to drop, is contentious and emotionally charged. Even the International Energy Agency, which advocates for accessible and dependable energy sources for customers around the world, declared in July 2007 that global oil production will eventually peak and then fall irreversibly. This prediction is still disputed in some circles today. The effects this might have on our daily lives are impossible to foresee.

The law of simple economics will take over and the price of oil will rise if supply cannot meet demand. The most noticeable and immediate impact might be the rationing of fuel, as described above, and the eventual rise in the cost of driving for the majority of people. In order to delay the peak oil disaster and start implementing the fundamental lifestyle adjustments that may be required in the near future, we must start reducing travel today and sourcing more goods locally. One day it may be necessary rather than optional to live and work in the same place.

Who is Eligible to Work Remotely?

Many duties in some professions may be completed using a phone or computer, thus these jobs are good candidates for working from home. Since you can use your abilities everywhere you can carry and connect a computer, anyone in the IT field has an advantage over others when it comes to working from home. Similar factors make it simple to perform sales and marketing tasks from home.

More individuals are now able to work from home thanks to the most recent advancement in call centres.

Call centres were once operated from a sizable, central site in the UK, but later, through a process known as "offshoring," the work was relocated to nations like India where labour is far less expensive. Customers service positions are now being "home shored" and made available to UK residents who live from home and have flexible schedules by businesses in sectors that demand a thorough understanding of their market. The largest "virtual contact centre" in the UK is maintained by Co-op Travel Group, which also employs over 600 remote workers.

Despite having a UK office, Texperts hires employees from all around the world to respond to the text inquiries that their clients send in.

NOT ALL JOBS CAN BE COMPLETED FROM HOME

There are certainly some tasks that cannot and will never be completed from home. If you work as a nurse, a truck driver, or a cook in a restaurant, you cannot work from home. There may be supplies and equipment held at your workplace that cannot be transported to your home. You might also require frequent face-to-face interactions with clients and co-workers in your place of business.

However, there are some situations when it may be absolutely feasible to restructure your workday such that you spend some time at home and the remainder at the office or out with clients. Or

You may give your current abilities a fresh spin and work from home as a freelancer to put them to use. From his kitchen at home, a chef may provide catering for parties or create a variety of dishes to sell to restaurants and grocery stores. Using a spare room as his office, the truck driver may launch a courier service. Whether you need to work out a deal with your boss to allow you to work from home, find a means to earn money from home through self-employment, or launch a small business, we examine how to get started as a homebody in Chapter 3.

What makes working from home so beneficial?

In spite of numerous rejections and a gruelling three-hour interview, Sarah, a sales professional who works from home in a distant rural area, was so certain that working from home was her best option that she persisted for a year before finding a company prepared to give her a chance. Working from home is something that many of the folks I spoke with while conducting research for this book are really excited about. What precisely do we value so highly? There are advantages for businesses, for the community, and for the environment, in addition to advantages for you personally. Listed below are the benefits in my opinion.

BENEFITS OF WORKING FROM HOME

- If you work, you can cut costs on things like transportation, child care, buying and dry-cleaning work clothes, drinks, snacks, and impulsive purchases.

- Avoiding the struggle to go to work and return saves you hours every day. With that extra time, you can do whatever fits you best—sleep in, organize your life, play with the kids, clean, etc.

- When you're not distracted by co-workers and office activities, you can do more high-quality work.

- Don't fret about dealing with traffic and avoiding risky drivers on the highway, or about getting caught in traffic and arriving late while taking public transportation.

- Your career options are improved when you are not restricted to occupations requiring commuting. See Chapter 3 for further details on Sarah's journey from receiving a modest salary to being the family's principal breadwinner by locating a job she could do from home. You can still earn a living or some additional money even if you are limited to your home, and you can keep your job even if you move hundreds of miles away.

- You are in charge of creating your own life. You are more independent and flexible at home. Nobody is going to tell you when to go for coffee or when to return after lunch. You can take business calls after hours or personal calls during business hours and work when you are naturally more productive.

- You can take the first available appointment to see the doctor and dentist by being at home when a delivery or workman is scheduled to arrive "any time between 9 a.m. and 5.30 p.m." Getting time off for the school play and sports day is no longer a challenge. There may be opportunity for community events.

- Due to the lack of appealing coffee shops, sandwich bars, and birthday cream cakes, you may even get fitter, leaner, and healthier. Between jobs, you can squeeze in some exercise to help your body and mind.

BENEFITS OF WORKING FROM HOME FOR BUSINESES

- By not needing to house as many employees, property costs and overheads are decreased. Microsoft has reportedly encouraged flexible working for its employees, and by doing so, has been able to add 400 extra employees to its Reading headquarters. By delaying the construction of new premises by two years, the business has already saved nearly £1 million annually.

- Small businesses that operate from home save money on the high costs of commercial mortgages, rent, and utilities.

- Employers are able to recruit highly skilled and motivated employees by demonstrating that they are forward-thinking and receptive to innovation.

- Employers find it simpler to keep these top-notch employees and save money on pricey hiring and training costs.

- In the face of fierce domestic and international rivalry, all these savings increase competitiveness.

- Having someone in the house all day or portion of it provides security for you, your neighbours, and them.

- If people are in your neighbourhood all day and need to use the services available there, your neighbourhood becomes livelier. Paper and stamps are purchased by home schoolers from their neighbourhood newsstand. Ideally, they have the time and desire to shop for their food locally as well, preserving small grocery stores that would otherwise be displaced by out-of-town superstores.

- During the typical rush hours, the roadways become less crowded. Consider how different it is when schools are out of session. How much more peaceful would the streets be if up to 50% of the working population worked from home?

DIFFERENCES BETWEEN HOME WORKING AND OFF-SITE WORK

- Homeworkers who cut down on their work kilometres minimize their carbon emissions into the atmosphere.

- To save utility costs, lower the thermostat, improve insulation, and turn off computers and appliances.

- Spend part of the time they would have spent commuting shopping locally or perhaps growing their own fruits and veggies.

Negative Effects of Working from Home

The idea of working from home is not one that everyone finds appealing, it must be noted. Boris Johnson stated that "the office is the natural habitat of Homo sapiens" and "working from home is simply a euphemism for sloth, apathy, staring out of the window and random surfing of the internet" in an article about public transportation and the horrors of commuting in the Daily Telegraph in July 2007. I've also read a reaction to a piece of writing on the internet where the author said that anyone who can work from home full-time must have a job that is meaningless.

These outbursts are undoubtedly intended to spark discussion, but there is always a cost associated with anything, therefore I think it's best to start by discussing the drawbacks of homeworking. What's the cost of all these fantastic advantages of working from home?

DISADVANTAGES OF WORKING FROM HOME

- You lose regular communication with co-workers when you work from home, which could make you feel lonely. All the homeworkers I spoke to while conducting research for this book emphasized this negative aspect of doing homework. You probably won't be content working from home unless you're ready to acknowledge that it's totally up to you to figure out your own means of overcoming loneliness and developing a network of allies.

- On the other hand, having more contact with your family could lead to conflict if you can't set mutually acceptable boundaries and uphold them.

- It could be challenging for you to organize your workday in a productive manner.

- If you spend all of your time in one place, you could feel constricted and lose out on your co-workers, a change of scenery, and local shops and eateries.

- When no one else is there to observe your work, it can be challenging to retain the self-discipline needed to maintaining a consistent pace.

- On the other side, some people find it difficult to unwind when work is so close by; you risk developing a workaholic addiction to your "Crack Berry."

PROBLEMS WITH WORKING FROM HOME IF YOU ARE ALSO AN EMPLOYEE

- You may find yourself working extra hard (skipping breaks and working long hours) merely to prove that you are pulling your weight because office-based co-workers may be resentful of those working from home and view it as an unfair advantage open to skiving.

- Managers may occasionally be against the notion if they worry that output will suffer in terms of quality and quantity.

- As more employees work from home, managers may view it as a benefit that should be saved for themselves or worry about losing their own employment.

- When your co-workers believe that "it's okay for some," you might not receive much assistance for the difficulties of doing your schoolwork, such as phone and internet issues and feelings of isolation.

- Effective communication must be set up to prevent team morale from suffering if you are not all there at the same time, share knowledge, and maintain the consistency of your output.

- You must put in a lot of effort to continue to be on decision-makers' minds if you desire a promotion.

DISADVANTAGE OF WORKING FROM HOME FOR SELF-EMPLOYED

- It might be challenging to build a home-based business and grow your clientele if you have no visible presence in the community.

- Because you are removed from major commercial areas, your ability to get business information and guidance will be based on how well you are able to explore what is accessible in your neighbourhood.

Is Working from home for me?

I hope this has given you a realistic understanding of the problems with homeworking. Without exception or prodding, every homeworker I spoke to stated that while working from home has its drawbacks, they believed the benefits outweighed the drawbacks and they wouldn't want to work any other way. This book's goal is to help you minimize the disadvantages while maximizing the benefits. Do you think you might choose to work from home now that you've read about them both? And if so, how near are you to attaining it?

Chapter 2

CAN I WORK FROM HOME AND BE SUCCESSFUL?

No matter what kind of business you do, working from home has its own special requirements that you must be able to meet while also performing your job properly. People I spoke with throughout my research for this book often stated that they thought particular qualities were necessary for working remotely.

Self-discipline and self-motivation are the ones that are most frequently stated and that new home schoolers appear to be most concerned about. Even though no one is watching you and no one may know how much you are accomplishing, it is crucial to be able to encourage yourself to start working and stay going until you have completed each task.

Of course, it's difficult to predict how self-disciplined and motivated you would be when working from home if you're used to working with others until you give it a try if you're used to teamwork. Finding out about some important facets of your personality is the greatest place to start when determining whether you are suitable for working from home. If you already do your research, this knowledge will assist you in understanding who you are and what is preventing you from succeeding more.

The following paragraphs offer some basic perceptions about your personality:

1. How several characteristics affect your effectiveness as a homeworker
2. How you interpret the world—whether you are a visual, auditory, or
   kinaesthetic type—and how understanding your type can improve your ability to learn, connect with others, and express gratitude.
4. What drives you—are you motivated to move toward something or away from
   something?
5. Do you view time and schedules from an in-time or through-time perspective?
6. Do you tend to be proactive or reactive while making decisions?
7. Fill out the form to see how you might react to working from home.

If your brain is currently wired in a way that is advantageous for working from home, you will learn how it is made up. You'll pick up some techniques for managing situations more skilfully if there's room for improvement.

With this level of self-awareness, you can look at yourself with objectivity and recognize when you need to make adjustments. You can then alter your behaviour to get greater achievements thanks to self-discipline and self-motivation. If you are adaptable and open-minded, working from home might be a crash course in learning more about who you are.

Why Character Matters

Employers frequently use personality testing, also known as personality profiling, and you may have already done one as part of the hiring, promotion, or training process. The most popular personality assessments in business involve a series of questions about your behaviour preferences and the use of your answers to place you on four indices. In his research on psychological preferences and how they influence people's ways of dealing with life, German psychologist Carl Jung developed three of these in the 1920s. The fourth was afterwards included.

By checking the boxes next to the following items, you can now learn more about your preferences for extraversion or introversion, intuition or sensing, thinking or feeling, and judging or perceiving. You will learn how each influences your performance as a homeworker, and in each section, I offer advice as to how each type may increase their pleasure and performance when working from home, even though your responses might not neatly fit into one category or the other. You may be able to balance this feature of your personality and manage the aspects of homeworking related to it if you check the same number of questions for each type.

BOTH INTROVERT AND EXTROVERT

The Latin words "extra," which means outside, "intro," which means inside, and "vertebra," which means to turn, are where Jung got the names "extroversion" and "introversion" from. Therefore, an extrovert looks to the outside, frequently to other people, for inspiration whereas an introvert looks within, to their own resources. Asking yourself these questions will reveal whether you have an introverted or extroverted personality.

Do you

a. change after a long day at work and go to the bar to spend the evening catching
   up with friends?
b. frequently speak before completely considering what you want to say?
c. have a large circle of friends and acquaintances?
d. after a long day at work, spend a calm evening at home with a good book or
   your preferred television shows?
e. frequently hears compliments on your listening skills?
f. does you only confide in a select group of close friends?

You have extrovert tendencies if the answers to questions a) through c) were yes. You seek out company and gain energy from it.

If you selected "yes" to questions d) through f), you may be an introvert.

The Outgoing Type

Extroverts enjoy a lot of action and don't require a lot of downtime for reflection. If working from home is to be successful and enjoyable for you, you will need to maintain a strong support network because you may find working alone to be tedious and demoralizing due to your love of company. On the plus side, you usually have greater freedom to do this at home than in a typical office setting.

The Reserved Personality

If you're an introvert, you receive your energy from within, therefore you can discover that other people drain you. You prefer to be independent and lonely, and you are fascinated by concepts and ideas. Working from home will appeal to you if you enjoy being by yourself, but you will still require social interaction. Limiting the number and duration of meetings you schedule to give yourself plenty of reflection time afterward may help you gain the greatest networking benefits.

Managing loneliness

Given that isolation is frequently cited as the biggest obstacle to working from home, it's clear that your level of extroversion or introversion will have a significant influence on how comfortable you feel doing so. However, working from home is still an option even if you are an extrovert. It essentially comes down to understanding your own needs and changing your routines to suit them. In fact, it's so crucial that I've spent the entirety of Chapter 7 to discussing isolation and how to maintain connections even when working alone.

Nobody is fully extrovert or entirely introverted, of course; we all fall somewhere along a sliding spectrum, and depending on the situation, we may go up or down the scale. When spending time with family or familiar friends, an introvert may be the life of the party; however, an extrovert may dread the idea of attending a gathering where they know no one.

If there is enough incentive, we can also teach ourselves to deal with circumstances that are outside of our comfort zone, such as when our jobs require us to entertain clients.

Sometimes people are so skilled at acting that when they admit it was all an act and not at all who they really were, other people are shocked.

PERCEPTION AND INSTINCT

Jung used the phrases "sensing" and "intuition" to describe how people process information and perceive the outside world. The following questions will help you determine whether your preferred mode of perception is sensing or intuition.

Do you

a) think of yourself as practical and grounded?
b) exhibit a preference for the small print over the broader picture?
d) Do you enjoy seeing concrete results?
d) consider yourself to be receptive to intuition and inspiration?
e) would rather focus on the large picture than the specifics?
f) find it challenging to complete routine work?

You are what Jung called a sensing type if you checked yes to questions a) to c).
You are perceptive if you selected yes to questions d) through f).

As the name implies, sensing types greatly rely on what their five senses are giving them and believe this knowledge because it is based on their own first-hand experience. They value order and systems and are engaged in the present moment. Those that are intuitive are more interested in their "gut sensations" and the motivation they might offer. They have a passion for the future, are receptive to new ideas, and are more inclined to be innovators.

THE SENSING TYPE

Since you naturally concentrate on the day-to-day, practical aspects of doing your work, if you are the perceptive kind, you tend to adapt well to homeworking. You create your own systems and implement checks to double-check that processes take place at the appropriate times. You excel at planning, and you enjoy knowing that everything is in order. However, if you place too much focus on current efficiency, you could disregard long-term planning and be reluctant to seize chances that call for a risky move.

THE INFLUENTIAL TYPE

If you have an intuitive personality, you thrive in strategic thinking because you are a quick thinker who can switch your attention quickly from one idea to another. Since working from home requires you to focus more about the future than about the day-to-day operations, you tend to jump erratically from one task to another when you're bored with your normal tasks. If you do your assignments at home, you might want to think about getting assistance with rote chores like correspondence and record-keeping.

THEORY AND EMOTION

The various forms of information we consider when making judgments are related to thinking and feeling. Answer the following questions to learn more about your decision-making process:

Do you

a) base your choices on factual data?
b) make a point for the sake of logic rather than to maintain harmony?
c) would you rather tell the truth even if no one wants to hear it?
d) make decisions based on the emotions of others?
e) go above and beyond to fulfil the needs of others?
f) try to stay out of a fight?

You are a thinking type if you selected yes to questions a) through c).
You are a feeling type if you indicated yes to questions d) to f).

THE THINKING TYPE

If you are a thinking person, you base your decisions on factual knowledge. Your priority is finishing the task at hand, not getting along with the people involved or worrying about their possible emotional reactions. You must bear in mind to schedule time to stay in touch with others when working from home, solely for their own reason. The occasional fast phone call or email, regardless of how busy you are to make sure everything is fine will keep co-workers on board for when there is an emergency and you, the thinker, need their assistance.

THE EMOTIONAL TYPE

If you are an emotional person, you base your decisions on how you feel about something and how they will influence other people. When working from home, you must exercise self-control to avoid talking on the phone for an extended period of time to check in with your co-workers. Try to focus on your own objectives rather than worrying too much about what other people think or feel. Avoid getting sucked into other people's troubles at all costs. Having a confidant who is familiar with your line of work will aid you in maintaining perspective.

APPRAISAL AND JUDGMENT

A mother-daughter pair of psychologists known as Myers Briggs expanded on Jung's three indicators by adding a fourth in the 1940s, turning his theories into the still-commonly-used approach to analysing personality. How people react to their surroundings is examined by the judging and perceiving scale.

Answer the following questions to determine which type you are.

a) Are you organized and prefer to plan your life?
b) decide what to do and follow through on it?
c) Are you proud of your persistence in getting things done?
d) enjoy being flexible and impulsive?
e) prefer to have options available to you?
You take pride in being adaptable, right?

You are a judge if you responded positively to questions a) through c).
Perceivers are those who provided yes answers to questions d) through f).

Being able to balance your judging and perceiving tendencies is necessary for being a successful home schooler. The judge allows you to take advantage of the freedom that working from home brings, whether it comes in the form of unforeseen good weather or a social visit, and the perceiver can allow you to be spontaneous and take advantage of those freedoms. You can also enjoy the time off knowing that you can rely on yourself to make up any lost time.

LEVEL OF PERCEPTION

When working from home, deadlines can be difficult if you are a perceiving personality because they limit your options and restrict your freedom. To handle this, you might need to come up with your own plan.

Regardless of how far away the deadline is, a homeworker I know takes delight in submitting work as soon as he can. This way, he never has to worry about deadlines!

JUDGEMENT TYPE

The self-discipline and organization that others find so challenging to manage won't be a problem for you if you are the judging kind who works from home. You've carefully thought out a strategy, and you follow it. Don't let possibilities pass you by failing to see them if they don't fit into your plan, and avoid becoming too fixed in your thinking to avoid losing some of your originality.

Why Different People Have Different Perspectives

- Our awareness of what we are seeing (visual sense), hearing (auditory sense), and physically feeling at any given time depends on the five various ways that the brain processes information.

- (Kinaesthetic perception), smelling (olfactory perception), or taste (gustatory sense). The first three, visual, auditory, and kinaesthetic, are crucial when working from home:

- The visual sense enables you to perceive what is going on around you, such as individuals passing by, as well as the images you are conjuring up in your thoughts.

- Your aural sense allows you to hear both what you are saying to yourself and sounds from the outer world, such as passing vehicles.

- The kinaesthetic sense offers external bodily experiences like the rain on your face and internal bodily feelings like hunger.

While you use each sense individually to perceive the environment, you frequently have a preferred or predominate sense. People who work from home will find it helpful to know if they are more visual, auditory, or kinaesthetic because it will assist them organize their workspace and comprehend their unique working habits.

By carefully observing the language you frequently employ, you can determine which senses you and other people prefer. Saying "I see what you mean," for instance, indicates that your visual system is being used. I can hear what you're saying indicates that the auditory system is dominant. I feel out of touch implies that the kinaesthetic system is dominant. You can have a system that you use the most, closely followed by another. I didn't realize how often I respond when someone suggests a plan with "I'll see how I feel" (visual, kinaesthetic) until it was pointed out to me.

Because of my keen sense of sight, I become easily agitated when my desk and office are disorganized.
I know it sounds compulsive, but I simply can't do any work until I have cleaned up and organized myself. Those who prefer the aural sense can detest working in a noisy setting or somewhere where they might be disturbed. People who are more kinaesthetic may have strong opinions about the type of workstation and chair they use and need to be relaxed before they can concentrate. When setting up your home office, all of these things should be taken into account.

HOW TO UNDERSTAND YOUR LEARNING

Our primary sense also has a significant impact on how we learn. Knowing how we learn best is essential for those of us who do their homework because, in most cases, we are responsible for learning new material on our own, frequently in a short amount of time.

Educating the visual learner

E-learning programs will work for you because you learn best by being able to see instructions or an illustration. I can absorb knowledge much more quickly if I can read it or see it for myself. People reading to me from the newspaper slows down my understanding process, thus I detest it.

The Auditory Type of Learning

The most effective way to learn is to hear a lecture or verbal instructions, therefore eLearning maybe helpful, with a strong aural component. You can listen in the car while listening to tapes and CDs, which are especially convenient if you're short on time. You will hear a tremendous amount of information even when not paying attention.

Training for Kinaesthetic Learners

To learn a new skill, you will need to use the necessary tools and perform the necessary steps yourself. Have you ever tried watching someone else perform a new computer task to learn how to do it yourself? Even though I have a strong visual sense, my kinaesthetic sense lags behind, therefore I find it frustrating and difficult to understand when someone else explains a program to me, whether in a lecture or one-on-one setting. The mouse is beckoning me to grab hold of it and click it where it needs to be.

Therefore, if you are having trouble understanding anything, attempt to find it in a format that closely resembles the type of learning that you prefer instead of beating yourself up about being stupid (s). You are likely to understand it much more quickly if the information is presented in a different way.

Understanding Your Interpersonal Relationships

Since you frequently work alone when working from home, it is crucial for you to build and maintain strong working relationships and not rely on PAs or co-workers to do it for you. You can obtain a sense of your co-workers' and clients' favoured types by paying close attention to what they have to say. (However, keep in mind that we all have senses, and the one we utilize most often can vary depending on our mood and the circumstances.)

You are less likely to leave a conversation with someone feeling as though no meaningful communication had taken place, even though you both understood every word that was spoken. You'll quit attempting to get them to "see" something that they just weren't "hearing"! Additionally, you might discover that your bonds with clients, suppliers, and co-workers grow considerably stronger over time.

KNOWING WHEN AND HOW TO SAY THANK YOU

When our attempts to treat others as we would like to be treated ourselves don't always produce the anticipated results, we are left perplexed and may even feel hurt and rejected. You can make advantage of the thorough insight and knowledge you have through interacting directly with people as a homebody.

Gratitude To Visual Learners

The visual-oriented co-worker will appreciate seeing your appreciation for their participation. A thank-you card or a bouquet of flowers they can display will be appreciated. Always dress appropriately whenever you see them since you should keep in mind how important appearance is to them.

Acknowledging Auditory People

It may be important for others to hear how well they are doing, not just through the words they speak but also via the tone of voice. To casual or caustic remarks, they could be quite sensitive.

Thanks to the kinaesthetic kinds

Don't be startled if you receive a hug from a co-worker when you were hoping for a handshake; kinaesthetic personalities may be more prone than others to show physical affection in professional settings.

WHY DO YOU GET OUT OF BED IN THE MORNING?

One of the most common concerns about working from home is lack of motivation.
One frequently asked question is, "How do I know I won't spend the entire day in my pyjamas watching television?" Although I believe most people find the necessity to pay the mortgage and please their boss or clients to be fairly pressing, the question is still valid.

Understanding your fundamental motivations—as opposed to just the strain of making ends meet and, perhaps, having some spending money left over—will be a big assistance to you after reading this section. The problem of finishing work while working alone at home should become less of a concern once you realize this. You'll also gain a better understanding of why some people behave in a particular way, which may help you prevent future conflicts arising from disparate patterns. Since we are all complex individuals who do not neatly fit into boxes, read the questions below and consider the type of person you normally fall into. To fully analyse your responses, you might want to write them down.

WHAT INSPIRES YOU?

Let's take remote employment as an illustration. Consider the reasons you already

work from home, or the motivations behind your consideration of it.

What do you hope to accomplish and what matters most to you?

Do you want to escape the monotony of your everyday commute, for instance?

Perhaps you don't need to deal with office politics and distractions. Maybe you feel guilty using so much of your hard-earned money for travel.

Do you believe working from home would improve the quality of your life? Or would you want to spend more time with your spouse or kids? Maybe you think that if you can make all your own food, you can lead a healthier lifestyle.

After you've listed your personal justifications for working from home, take another look at the list of possible justifications in the first paragraph above. Here is a list of items you should

dislike, and a desire to "get away from." The items you like and want to "advance toward" are listed in the second paragraph. Take a look at what you wrote. Do you want to get rid of them or are they things you wish to avoid? Or are they the things you actually want, the ones you want to pursue? Try reflecting on other parts of your life, such as your choice of home, vacation destination, and pals, if you're unsure which dominates in this situation. Do you frequently choose actions that will help you move away from things you dislike or toward things you like? To choose goals that motivate you, you only need to be aware of the strategy you naturally like.

INSPIRED AWAY FROM

In the old "carrot and stick" paradigm, the person who is typically "away from" will react better when offered something they detest and desire to flee from.

To put it another way, from the stick. The need to perform well enough to avoid termination or to stay away from people, places, and things they detest will serve as their motivation.

PUSHING FORWARD

Promises of a wage raise or promotion will be more motivating to them because they respond better to the "carrot" than the normally "toward" person. A person who is "toward" you won't be motivated by the threat of something bad; instead, they will become irate.

When you need to get something done, keep an eye out for this in other people's conversations as well. When it comes to the "carrot or stick" situation, the trick is in knowing when to use the carrot or the stick!

HOW DO YOU MAINTAIN TIME?

When you work from home and there is no one to keep track of the time for you, knowing how you think about time might be a useful indicator of how well you are likely to be able to manage your time. What kind of person are you in terms of managing your time?

ARE YOU CONSISTENTLY LATE OR ARE YOU ALWAYS ON TIME?

Do you frequently glance at the clock and generally have an idea of the time? Do you enjoy keeping your appointments? Are you still conscious of the passage of time and the next appointment in your calendar even if you may be focusing on one activity at a time?

Or perhaps you have a tendency to become so engrossed in what you are doing that you lose track of time. You might inform your colleague that you are about to accomplish something, get distracted by another task, then another, and forget what you were doing initially.

You surely recognize these many perspectives on time, and perhaps they motivate you. 'Through-time' refers to the first person, and 'in-time' refers to the second. People who are "through-time" are always on time and dislike having to wait for their "in-time" friends who are always running behind schedule and arrive exhausted from all the things they got caught up in.

APERTURES OF TIME

Working from home is more likely to help people manage their time more effectively. You'll be able to schedule time in order to finish particular chores while keeping in mind what will come next as you become more aware of how time is going. Try arriving a little later than expected if you are meeting someone who will arrive on time, or bring a book so you won't have to wait around while they arrive.

TIMELY PEOPLE

When working from home, people must use time management techniques.

You may set a reminder on your phone or alarm to get a new job.

You get bored with a task more quickly than through-time folks, so attempt to work on it for an additional ten minutes when you start to get tired of it. You'll accomplish far more this way. If you have trouble setting priorities, list all of your tasks in exact order of importance (more on this in Chapter 5, page 88), then adhere to it, only going on once you have finished each one.

Decision After Decision

If a decision needs to be taken when working from home, no one else will be there to direct you. This section will assist you in determining whether you have trouble making decisions and what kind of work suits you as a homebody the best. Which of the following best describes your perspective on decision-making?

- Do you put off making a decision until you absolutely have to? Would you want to let others decide what should occur?

- Or do you want to act without thinking first and take matters into your own hands? Do you dislike bureaucracy?

RESPONSE AND ACHIEVEMENT

You are a "reactive" person if the first description of yourself is a good fit for you. A "proactive" individual who excels at completing tasks is described in the second description.

Your type may be revealed by the type of work you do — proactive types make good salespeople; reactive types are adept at studying and analysing. Consider the professions and acquaintances you have. Would you please categorize them?

There are many occupations where your management or other variables dictate your work flow, or where you are needed to answer to an external demand, such as telephone inquiries flowing into your office, so just because you tend to be reactive doesn't imply you shouldn't work from home. However, if you're considering going into business for yourself, you should be aware that it will require a higher level of being proactive or learning to be so. In some circumstances, you might already be assertive.

We frequently behave differently at home than at work, for instance, and merely need to become used to using that strength in a different setting.

Chapter 3

AM I ABLE TO WORK FROM HOME?

You might be wondering if it is really possible to stay at home and still earn a living considering how common it has grown over the past century or so to go to work outside the home. In many instances, the answer to that question is "yes," and if it isn't right now, with a little bit of preparation and effort, it might be in the not-too-distant future.

This chapter addresses:

1. A warning regarding widely publicized "opportunity" for doing homework.
2. Things to consider if you already have a job but want to work from home.

3. How to convince your supervisor to let you work from home.
4. Numerous strategies for working from home as a freelancer.
5. Handling the bureaucracy of self-employment.
6. A few fundamental guidelines for handling finances when working for yourself.
7. Who to turn to for assistance when working for yourself.

"Opportunity" for doing homework.

Many people find the prospect of earning a little more money at home appealing, whether it is between domestic and family responsibilities or after work. In order to make a quick money, con artists that prey on people's insecurities have a sizable market. You've probably seen advertisements that read something like "Earn £1000 a day working part time from home" plastered to lampposts at busy traffic intersections, displayed in the back of a car, or placed in the jobs section of the local newspaper.

Or perhaps you have seen the advertisements on search engine websites promising large earnings "with a cast-iron guarantee" for running an internet business or have gotten unwanted emails. These advertisements are deliberately crafted to appeal to those who are a little strapped for cash and would welcome the opportunity to earn some quick money. They prey on people's tendency to believe in something that seems like a simple, quick solution to a problem without giving the details much thought. Is it unreasonably appealing? In such case, sadly, it is unreal.

Alarm bells should go off if an advertisement seems credible, but when you inquire further, you are required to send money upfront, either as a registration fee or to purchase stock. Have you ever been required to make a payment to apply for a job? I don't think so. Someone is attempting to defraud you if a payment is requested.

Visit www.homeworking.com for more details on how to recognize homeworking scams and to read about other people's experiences. The website has a forum where you can post your own experiences and request user feedback.

Is working remotely for a company the appropriate move?

Before selecting to work remotely, there are numerous aspects to think about, including your own goals, your situation, and those of your employers. Just because you are employed by someone else does not mean that you cannot work from home. If you present the concept to your supervisor in the appropriate manner, they may just not have considered it themselves and be receptive to the possibility. Here are some factors to consider as you evaluate the suggestion.

IS WORKING FROM HOME A GOOD OPTION FOR MY PROFESSIONAL AND PERSONAL GOALS?

Working from home has drawbacks, as we saw in Chapter 1, one of which is that you unavoidably lose some of your visibility with co-workers and superiors. Consider whether working from home may hurt your chances of getting promoted if you're ambitious and want to further your career. Does Chapter 6's discussion of strategies to stay in touch with your co-workers and superiors provide you with enough exposure to help you advance your career?

WHAT IS BEST FOR MY FAMILY AND HOME ENVIRONMENT ABOUT WORKING FROM HOME?

If you don't live alone in blissful seclusion, you'll need to think about how working from home will affect your family and home life. If you share a residence with others, you may have trouble finding the time and space to focus on your work if you have diverse working schedules or don't work.

How can taking care of youngsters or elderly relatives fit along with working from home? What will take place throughout the summer break?

Before you start working from home, it's important that your family understands how the change will affect them and how they can help it go well. How to do this with your partner and kids is covered in Chapter 8.

CAN I APPLY FOR A WORK FROM HOME DECISION FROM MY EMPLOYER?

Any employee may request flexible working conditions from their company. These conditions may include job sharing, modifying working hours, taking holidays during particular times of the year, or—most intriguingly for our purposes—working from home one day a week. However, parents of children under the age of six, parents of disabled children under the age of 18, and caregivers of some adults have the right to request their employers allow them to work flexibly, and employers are required by law to give such requests serious consideration (note that this obligation only applies to consider, not necessarily to grant). The administration has also made plans to expand this privilege to all workers who have children under the age of sixteen.

The worker is required to show that the sought flexible working conditions are feasible and won't harm the company. The request must be taken into account, and the employer has the right to refuse it if, for instance, it would result in additional expenses, have a detrimental effect on business performance, or alter how other employees are organized for work.

The Resources section at the conclusion of this chapter provides a link to the Department of Business Enterprise and Regulatory Reform's (DBERR) website, which provides detailed information on your rights, the employer's obligations, and the process to file a complaint.

follow, along with sample applications for flexible working. But in order to have the best chance of being accepted for your application to work from home, you must first carefully consider your personal situation to determine whether it is a viable alternative for you.

DO I HAVE A CHANCE OF WORKING FROM HOME WITHIN MY COMPANY?

As we have shown, even if you may ask for flexible working, your employer has the right to reject your request if they feel there are compelling business justifications for doing so.

After speaking with a number of home employees about how they were able to work out their bosses' willingness to allow them to do their work from home, it appears that there are two key elements at work here. One is the company's culture and willingness to adapt, and the other is you and your interactions with your supervisor and co-workers.

Occupational culture

You may find it more challenging to persuade your employer of the advantages of working from home if you work for a company with an outdated outlook, which I define as a highly structured organization with a defined hierarchy and its own bureaucratic way of doing things. Instead, then focusing on the work that employees do and whether this can be accomplished elsewhere, a traditional organization may still prioritize employees' physical presence in the workplace. There can be reservations regarding the volume, calibre, and timeliness of the work you will be doing, especially if you are the first person to request the ability to work from home.

Seeing all the advantages of cost-cutting, increased productivity, and enhanced morale outlined in Chapter 1, some businesses have embraced homeworking with zeal. After beginning with 400 teleworkers ten years ago, BT is now a recognized leader. BT today employs 12000 employees who work from home, and 63,000 of them are part of some type of flexible working arrangement. If working from home is your ultimate aim, it will pay to do some research and ask questions about potential employers' views on working from home every time you apply for a position.

Your professional standing

This is the real meat of the issue. No matter how modern and enlightened your employers are, there is no way they will even consider the possibility of you working from home if you have a reputation for sloppy work, bad time management, or trouble getting along with clients and co-workers. They'll want to keep you in plain view at all times. On this one, it's up to you to be frank and brutally honest with yourself. In the event that before considering the concept of working from home, resolve any issues you may have had in the past and make sure you are in good standing.

On the other hand, if you are a valued employee, your managers could be unexpectedly accommodating in an effort to keep you.

IS IT EASY FOR ME TO WORK FROM HOME?

Answering that question should not be too difficult. In order to be able to work from home, you can think about trading your office-bound obligations with a co-worker.

How to convince your employer to let you work from home

However, at some point you'll need to sit down and speak with your supervisor. You might wish to use the DBERR template when creating your application for a home office job. Use these recommendations to give yourself the best chance of success.

- If you've put a lot of time and energy into the idea of working from home, you might feel a bit anxious about this talk. Despite the fact that you might feel as though a lot depends on this meeting, try to remain calm and approach it with the understanding that a good arrangement would benefit you both much. The reasons behind your request and how it would improve your work performance should be made clear.

- To demonstrate to your manager that you have given this some thought and are able to see things from their point of view as well, follow up with suggestions for how the arrangement could be implemented effectively. If you are prepared for potential criticism and have solutions to counter it, it will be beneficial.

- Give encouraging instances of other people you know who have successfully transitioned in a manner similar to your own, making sure to relate them as closely as you can to your own circumstance.

- Consider whether your suggestion has any consequences for cost-saving measures in advance. If fewer personnel are physically present, your organization may be able to save money on office space, heating and lighting costs, etc.

- Provide examples to demonstrate your willingness to be adaptable to the changing circumstances.

- Propose a trial period so the idea can be tried out and used to see how it performs. Or, test it out part-time with the idea that if it works, it will go full-time.
- Agree on the criteria you will use to judge the success of your plan: will it be output quantity or quality, keeping open lines of contact with other employees, or a factor specific to your position? By using an objective standard, you can prevent someone with biases against working from home or jealousy of you from jeopardizing the arrangement.

- It is advised to put your agreement in writing if you are not using the formal DBERR procedure (and there may be circumstances where a more informal approach is preferable). This will ensure that both parties are clear on what has been agreed upon, how long it will last, and how the results will be evaluated.

The next section is for you if you think the timing is right to start working for yourself.

As your own boss, you can earn money from home.

The number of persons who work from home who own their own firms is thought to be around two thirds. If you're a parent trying to balance work and family responsibilities, an employee facing layoffs, or someone who is just sick of the corporate grind, starting your own business from home is a tempting choice. The cost-effectiveness of starting a business from home allows you to test the market, determine whether there is a need for your good or service, and determine whether you are cut out for being your own boss.

It frequently turns out that being self-employed and managing a small business are completely different experiences than you anticipated. They require skills you would not have needed while you were employed by another person, like the courage to approach potential customers and close deals, the independence to make your own decisions, and the fortitude to persevere in the face of adversity. If you haven't read Chapter 2 yet, it covers aspects of self-awareness that can be helpful.

WHAT KIND OF BUSINESS COULD YOU START?

There are several methods to work for yourself, and not all of them need having a fantastic and ground-breaking new company idea. We'll go over each choice individually, and the Resources section at the end of the chapter has sources for extra information.

Using your existing knowledge

If you now use a talent or area of expertise as an employee, you can continue to do so as a self-employed person. I have heard folks state that they are tired of earning money for their job, thus they have made the decision to go it alone. In theory, this is a great idea, but before acting, you should thoroughly consider the financial ramifications of your choice. Otherwise, you can find yourself in a worse financial situation and possibly having to work more than ever. Later in this chapter, we examine the financial effects of working for yourself.

Franchise Acquisition

A franchise is the right to run a company that has already been established. Franchising is frequently viewed as a safer approach to start a business than from scratch because it has previously demonstrated success elsewhere. Toni and Guy hair salons, Kall-Kwik printers, and Clarks shoe stores are just a few examples of high street brands that run franchise operations. Items like operational manuals, stock, procedures, systems, and office supplies may be included in the franchise fee. All of this does, however, come with a cost, and you risk losing your money if the company fails. It pays to thoroughly investigate a franchise before deciding to join it, and you should always keep in mind that less scrupulous people are more concerned with getting their hands on your fee than with seeing you succeed.

Purchase of a Current Business

It may seem alluring to take over an established company, but in order to avoid buying a dud, you must conduct comprehensive research and properly negotiate the purchase price. Choose the type of business you want and the price range you can afford before you begin your search.

The national media, the internet, and print periodicals like Daltons Weekly all mention businesses that are for sale. By consulting your expert advisers, who are aware of the local business scene and may know of a company that is not being advertised, you may discover one. Finding out why the company is being sold is crucial, but it could be difficult to do so unless the owner is prepared to retire. When it comes to the fact that the company is not profitable, the owner could give any number of justifications.

As a result, you must conduct what is known as "due diligence," in which you analyse the entire company. An accountant can assist you in analysing the numbers, but you should also pay close attention to elements like procedures, important staff members, rivals, and market trends. Use the findings of your due diligence to bargain for a lower price because a business is only worth what someone is prepared to pay for it.

Direct selling, network marketing, multi-level marketing (MLM), and party planning
When a product is sold directly to the consumer, it is not through a retailer.

a middleman. Direct selling is a natural choice for mothers and employees who want to establish a small business while maintaining their day job because it can readily be done from home on a part-time basis. If you've ever had an Avon or Kleeneze brochure pushed through your door, you'll be aware that sales can be made door to door by leaving a catalogue and coming back later to collect orders. In addition, salesmen may approach their neighbours, friends, relatives, and other acquaintances in an effort to close a deal. They can also employ a party strategy, where they bring the goods along to friend gatherings for sample and demonstration before taking orders.

Network marketing, often known as multi-level marketing, may be a term you are familiar with (MLM). In other words, salesperson A sponsors or recruits person B to join the sales team and then receives a bonus based on B's sales as well as those of B's own network, or "downline," of salespeople. Network marketing organizations leverage the wealthy lifestyles of successful recruits to advertise their recruitment efforts since they may make a lot of money in the long run. How can you choose which company to join when all you see are pictures of enormous mansions and flashy cars? Anne, who joined a network marketing organization 18 months ago to supplement her retirement income and has since amazed herself with her professional and personal growth, assisted me in coming up with some rules. (I'm looking at this in detail because starting a network marketing business is much simpler and less expensive than buying a franchise or business, which requires extensive research, a sizable investment, and professional advice.) However, it may be more difficult to find unbiased advice when starting a network marketing business.

What to look for in a network marketing business

- Choose an organization that is reputable. To ensure that you can continue working hard to create the income you need now, you need to know that it will still be around in the future.
- Verify the company's business practices. To obtain a sense of how business is conducted and how people interact with one another and you, read the literature and attend the presentations.

- Choose a business with an expanding market. Consider the products the business sells and research its market share. Are more individuals interested in purchasing something, or is this a declining trend or industry?

- Choose your products wisely. You won't ever sell them to anyone unless they are of high quality, good value, and you enjoy using them yourself. The greatest choice is to sell consumables—items that are frequently consumed before being ordered again—as you can continue to grow your customer base in this way. You'll need to continuously find new customers if the products are one-time purchases.

- There is another factor that should be considered when determining whether a product is valuable: you have probably heard of pyramid schemes and are aware that they are prohibited. Since much of the money made in pyramid schemes is made through recruiting rather than selling actual goods, only those who join at the beginning are typically able to profit.

- I'm a new salesperson; how much help is accessible to me? To assist you in becoming productive rapidly, reputable network marketing businesses have created sophisticated training programs.

- If your sponsor is close by, it will be easier for you to meet up with them for support or to observe them at meetings and presentations.

- Verify the company's membership in the Direct Selling Association, a trade group with stringent ethical standards that all of its members are required to adhere to.

I also have a few recommendations for things to consider before making a decision based on my conversations with numerous people who have engaged in network marketing, both effectively and badly.

Things to think about before joining a network marketing business

- Network marketing is not a get-rich-quick plan, but it is possible to start earning little money right away.

- Network marketing is more advantageous for those who already own a business. They have both business and selling experience, in addition to an established clientele that would be interested in the products.

- Those who have achieved financial success have put in a lot of effort, time, and dedication. Be up front with your willingness to commit and how much time you have to spare.

- Regarding your objectives, you should be just as explicit. People join for a variety of reasons, such as to make extra money on the side, network with new people, or have money for retirement, but without a mutual understanding of your objectives, your sponsor won't be able to support you in reaching your objectives.

- While you do not need to be a polished "salesman" to be effective, you must love interacting with others. There is no way to transform an introvert into an extrovert by joining a network marketing organization. You might want to look at Chapter 2 right now if you haven't previously, which discusses how various personality types react to working from home.

- You must go past your usual "comfort zone" and do things that are initially uncomfortably uncomfortable if you want to be successful. But if you practice, those things will become natural to you, allowing you to venture further outside of your comfort zone. When engaging in network marketing, many individuals neglect this component of personal development.

- Even if you have a sponsor, you'll still need to find the will to study and do all the tasks you have to. There will be many ups and downs along the route, and you should be conscious of that from the beginning.

INTERNET-BASED BUSINESS

This can look like an alluring opportunity for the homeworker because press reports about a geek with an online concept becoming millionaire overnight frequently appear. The word "geek" in this context serves as a hint: it will be difficult unless you are passionate about IT and have the necessary skills, and hiring someone else to handle the technical aspects can be very expensive. If you have a great idea, you might consider collaborating with an IT expert, but keep in mind the considerations concerning partnerships mentioned below.

A website may appear like the best option if you are trying to increase the number of customers for products or services you are selling. However, merely adding yours to the millions of others already present in cyberspace will do nothing unless potential buyers can discover you in the first place and are then sufficiently pleased by the quality of your product to actually make a purchase. Both the design and programming necessary for the latter and the search engine optimization required for the former take a lot of time to learn and money to acquire. Successful websites take time and effort to build, so they shouldn't be thought of as a quick way to make money.

CONSIDERING A BUSINESS IDEA

People that are looking for something in particular launch many successful enterprises.

because they are dissatisfied that no one seems to offer their desired good or service and decide to provide it themselves. After trying to locate white bed linen and towels of great quality and reasonable price on the high street, Chrissie Rucker of The White Company did this in 1994. She initially packaged the orders from her twelve-page mail order brochure in a room at her boyfriend's house before being forced to move to a different location due to a lack of space. The White Company presently operates close to 20 stores, both domestically and abroad, and generates more than £50 million in revenue annually.

You could occasionally take an established business concept and give it a tiny twist by enhancing the product you sell or modernizing its appearance.

Keep an open mind to the chance that your initial concept might evolve into something you never would have anticipated. It's simple to get enamoured with your concept and want to follow it to the letter, but don't immediately write off a departure from your original course of action. You might discover that a fresh opportunity actually offers more mileage if you properly consider its long-term prospects.

Understanding the complexities of self-employment paperwork

Self-employed people always gripe about this part; as unpleasant as it may be, you now have to serve as an unpaid administrator for the government on top of running your business, delighting your clients, and keeping your books in order. The amount of official paperwork required when starting a new firm always astounded me in my interactions with people.

When it comes to business bureaucracy, ignorance is not an excuse. Regardless of what else is going on in your firm, you are required to learn what your legal obligations are and to fulfil them on time. Financial and legal repercussions may result if you don't.

All government agencies and organizations that offer business guidance, fortunately, offer a lot of assistance. However, you must inquire. You should be aware of the legal difficulties listed below, and the Resources section at the end of this chapter contains information on where you can receive more assistance on all of these topics. In case there are any additional legal concerns pertaining to credentials, licenses, continuous training, and other matters that are particular to your business, you should also double-check.

SELECTING YOUR BUSINESS'S STATUS

The legal status of your firm must be determined before you open for business since, at the most basic level, it impacts the type and amount of tax and National Insurance you will pay, whether you are personally liable for debts if the business fails, and the types of records you must keep. There are further repercussions, thus seeking impartial guidance from a business advisor, accountant, and/or legal is imperative before making a choice.

If you select one of the first three company structures (sole proprietorship, partnership, or limited liability partnership), you must register with Her Majesty's Revenue and Customs (HMRC) as a self-employed person; for further information on taxes, see the section below.

Individual Businessperson

Working alone and charging clients directly for your services as a sole proprietor is the easiest type of business to run. You could work as a dressmaker, decorator, consultant, gardener, writer, plumber, trainer, etc.

Partnership

With one or more other people, you may start a business together.
The costs of running the company and its earnings are divided among the partners.
They are all "jointly and severally accountable" for any debts the company accrues, which means you could be held responsible for the full amount owed if your partners fail to pay their fair share of the bills, either because they lack the funds or because they refuse to do so.

You should be extremely selective about who you enter into partnership with because business can present numerous possible points of contention. We've been pals for years; I've heard folks say so many times. They'll never let me down because I know them so well. We'll just deal with issues as they arise; there's no point in planning for problems before we even begin.

Such remarks always made me feel depressed. Before forming a partnership, talk through all the implications and sign a partnership agreement to gain insight into how you both view issues like finances, personal time, and individual obligations. What would you do if one of you wanted to leave? Who is accountable for the bank account? If your company is losing money, who bails you out? Even though it isn't comfortable to consider these scenarios at this optimistic moment, it is far preferable to do so now rather than later when time is of the essence. All these potentially controversial topics may be resolved objectively with the aid of a lawyer, who will also draft a legal agreement that spells out everyone's obligations. Working together is definitely not a smart idea if you can't come to a consensus at this point.

Limited Liability Partnership (LLP)

A limited liability partnership has a similar organizational structure to a partnership, but because each partner's liability is only limited by the amount of capital they have invested in the company, it is less financially hazardous if it encounters financial difficulties.

Limited Company

The fourth option is to 'incorporate' your firm at Companies House and operate it as a limited company, in which case the company is a separate legal entity from you and you are both a director and employee. This implies that you are not

In addition to being personally liable for corporate debts, being a director carries a host of other legal obligations, such as the annual filing of company accounts and annual filings with Companies House.

TAX

Within three months after beginning to work for yourself, you must register with Her Majesty's Revenue and Customs (HR&C) (or face a £100 fine) and let them know if you are forming a limited company. I'd advise getting in touch as soon as you consider opening a business because Revenue staff members offer free tax-related training across the nation, and it's best to be aware of your responsibilities as soon as possible. For those whose incomes may be unpredictable or who work in "certain occupations," leaflets are provided. These individuals may have various tax obligations from HMRC.

A tax self-assessment form must be filled out annually by sole proprietors, partnerships, and other business entities, whereas limited companies must need a licensed accountant to complete a more sophisticated tax form. The most important thing to keep in mind is that you need to save aside money throughout the year in order to pay your annual tax obligation in two instalments in January and July.

NATIONAL INSURANCE

To cover your state pension and other benefits, you must pay National Insurance contributions, which are also handled by HMRC. When you work as an employee, your employer withholds it from your compensation; but, if you work for yourself, you are responsible for paying it. Class 2 National Insurance contributions are made on a monthly or quarterly basis once you declare yourself as self-employed. You also have to pay Class 4 payments, which are a portion of your annual profit, if your profit surpasses a particular threshold.

VAT

Value Added Tax, also known as VAT, is levied on a number of goods and services in the UK. If your taxable turnover surpasses a certain threshold (£67,000 per year in the tax year 2008–09), you must register for VAT. If your turnover is less than the requirement, you may also register voluntarily. Once registered, you must include the correct tax rate on your invoices (the normal rate is 15% until the end of 2009), and you can then get a refund for any VAT you paid on the supplies and services you purchase for your company.

If you do not have your affairs in order, the VAT guy may be the bureaucracy that business owners fear the most because of his extensive powers. Keeping in mind that accounts in order and timely filing of returns, there is nothing to fear throughout the procedure, which is relatively simple. In fact, I've always considered having a VAT registration to be a unique benefit because it forces me to keep my books current.

HEALTH AND SECURITY

All enterprises, regardless of size, are subject to health and safety requirements, including those that are self-employed.

Small, and it's probable you'll need to register with the Health and Safety Executive or your Local Authority if you employ workers. To identify the risks associated with performing your job and put practical controls in place, you must conduct a risk assessment.

There are risks associated with working on ladders, lifting, using computers, electrical appliances, and cars, as well as loose computer and telephone lines that could trip someone.

There are also risks associated with working with toxic items (such as cleaning supplies). As a result, it is clear that no one or any profession can claim exemption. A written health and safety policy is required for employers with five or more employees.

ASSURANCE OF DATA

According to the Data Protection Act of 1998, any company that keeps personal data on its employees or clients, such as names, addresses, and other identifying information, should determine if it has to register with the Information Commissioner's Office as a data controller (ICO).

STAFF HIRING

It can make or break you to hire employees, which is a huge step for most small firms. In terms of hiring, paying, disciplining, and terminating employees, there is a colossal amount of legislation. As a result, I advise that you research your legal obligations as an employer before hiring anyone and carefully consider how much time and money it will take you to complete the hiring process (interviews, training, supervision, sick leave, etc.) as well as how much money it will cost you in wages and National Insurance (including holiday pay and maternity pay).

ENVIRONMENT

Finding out what the regulatory requirements are for your industry is important because the effect that all business activities have on the environment has grown significantly over the past few years. No business owner should complain to this bit of red tape because when you minimize waste and save resources, not only do you keep within the rules, but you may also save money and improve your reputation.

Taking care of your finances as a self-employed person

In my role as a business advisor, I discovered that although employed individuals frequently saw self-employment as a right to print money, the self-employed themselves strangely never hold that opinion. Self-employed people sometimes misjudge how long it will take for their new firm to begin bringing in money. I'd advise you to have enough cash on hand to cover your expenses for at least six months.

THE FINANCIAL REPERCUSSIONS OF BEING INDEPENDENT

The fact that self-employed people must pay all of their expenses before they can receive any income for themselves is conveniently disregarded in favour of the common misconception that they are entitled to large tax benefits. The remaining income needs to be set aside for the typical living expenses (mortgage or rent, bills, food, clothes, and spending money), tax, National Insurance, insurances, and a private pension.

If you run a sole proprietorship, it's likely that you won't make any money when you're not working, so you need to make enough money throughout the year to pay for your vacations and potential medical expenses.

I believe that the promise of these chances is what draws many people into self-employment, and their scarcity is what drives some back into the workforce. Considering that

Keep in mind that becoming self-employed has effects over a longer period of time than just this year and the following one. You can be considerably worse off as you near retirement if you don't have access to benefits like sick pay, holiday pay, and pension plans. It's a scary concept, to be sure, but the reality is that people frequently choose self-employment because it gives them so much more fulfilment than a traditional job that the financial benefits are actually incidental. If your ability to make ends meet is your top priority, finding and keeping a career you enjoy will make you happier than anything else.

FUNDING / GRANTS

There is a perplexing and ever-changing array of funding and grants available to entrepreneurs starting businesses, from bursaries granted by blue chip companies to European and government money aimed to assist revive areas of economic hardship.

The adage "there's no such thing as a free lunch" also holds true for "free money." You'll almost probably need to submit a reference during the application process.

Business plan that thoroughly and quantitatively details your anticipated performance; this type of forecasting takes time. You should be aware that the financing organization will need complete information of your trading data and projections of your future performance if funding is available and your application is accepted. This is because they now have a stake in your success. You can be asked to prominently display their logo on your materials or in your building and to take part in PR campaigns on their behalf. You may find this to be acceptable, but I have also heard of companies that, after going through the procedure, declined investment because they didn't like the terms and conditions.

In order to ensure that you are submitting all necessary information when applying for start-up money, attempt to contact a business advisor that can help you.

Applying For Financial Aid or Grants

Follow these suggestions to give yourself the best chance of success.

- Verify that you truly fulfil the eligibility requirements because funding organizations have a rigid policy regarding who is allowed to apply and the requirements they must meet. No matter how great your business idea, the funding organization will not "bend the rules a little bit."

- Even if you don't understand the request, thoroughly read the instructions and do it. Simply said, your application won't even be evaluated if it's incomplete.

- Resist the need to invent numbers for sales, expenses, profit, etc. Yes, it is challenging to estimate when you haven't even launched your business, however consider how much you can actually generate, how many clients you can serve in a day, how much you'll have to pay someone, etc.

- Conduct research to learn how much it will cost to make or supply your product or service, how much customers are likely to spend, and what the profit margin will be. Examine what is already being sold online, the price range, and talk to the customers who purchase your product. The staff members examining the applications are proficient with numbers, so they will be able to identify phony applications immediately quickly.

- Yes, all of this work is quite difficult, but that's the point. This organization may be giving you a large sum of money, and they want to make sure you are committed to using it wisely. If a friend didn't want to put in the effort to increase their chances of success, would you lend them money based on a whimsical idea?

LOANS

In the late 1990s and early 2000s, when the economy was booming, banks were flashing cash around, but since the credit crisis began in 2007, it has been more challenging to get loans, at least at reasonable interest rates. As it is tempting to take out a loan to fund stock, tools, premises, and other essentials during the riskiest years for young firms, this may actually be to their advantage. You can lessen your exposure to risk by renting, borrowing, or frugality.

Make sure your numbers add up and that you have adequate wiggle room between your income and expenses if you decide to apply for a loan. If required, get professional assistance. Also, avoid the pitfall of exaggerating your sales figures in order to, theoretically, be able to pay back loans. Your company may fall behind on bank payments and run the risk of going out of business if you are unable to maintain your predicted level of turnover.

INSURANCE

There is insurance available for every conceivable scenario, but when beginning a business, you often want to reduce expenditures to a minimal. To learn what regulations apply to your specific situation, research which types of business insurance are required by law. In the event that you harm someone or anything while performing your job, for instance, public liability insurance will protect you. It is a legal requirement to obtain employers' liability insurance if you have employees.

The simplest hazards to you and your company may also be something you want to insure. As we've seen, self-employed people cannot afford to be sick. If you can, consider purchasing private health insurance that will enable you to enter the hospital and return to work promptly. If you are out of work for a prolonged period of time—typically at least three months—a Permanent Health Insurance coverage will pay for your earnings. A policy may not pay out when you make a claim if you don't read the fine print on every one of them thoroughly to make sure they cover everything you require.

People you should be aware of while starting a business

Building a carefully chosen network of people who can give you advice and support is strongly advised because running a business may be a lonely experience. You should concentrate on your area(s) of expertise (often those that generate the greatest cash) and rely on others to offer specialized assistance. To do this, choose your advisors carefully.

While referrals from others are helpful, keep in mind that you and your company are unique and that a person who is really useful to a friend might not be as helpful to you. A potential adviser isn't the appropriate fit for you if you even feel a little uneasy around them. You must be able to ask them questions that seem silly to you and be confident that you will always receive a clear and understandable response. You will accomplish far more with the help of the top advisors than you ever could on your own. How to create your own informal and official support networks is covered in Chapter 7 as well.)

COMPANY ADVISOR

I have employed enterprise agency advisers for free, paid for advice on a private basis, and now serve as a business consultant both in the public and private sectors. As a result, I can speak on this topic from both sides of the argument.

As soon as you have a general concept of the type of business you want to launch, I advise you to locate your local Business Link or enterprise agency office and inquire about the resources available to you. Schedule a meeting and attend if free counsel is offered. At the very least, the business advisor will offer a variety of contacts and information, and at the absolute best, they will prove to be crucial in helping your firm get off the ground. They can suggest other counsellors for you or direct you to specialized organizations that can offer you more assistance. For instance, The Prince's Trust has a strong track record of offering financial and mentoring support to people of all ages.

Those between the ages of 18 and 30 who desire to launch their own business but are unemployed or underemployed PRIME assists others over 50 in doing the same.
A business advisor can assist you in developing a business plan, which is a technique to add some detail to the skeletal framework of your business idea. You need to be realistic about the amount of business you can expect to generate, your costs, your profit, the processes and time required, whether you need to hire staff, etc. You may need to reassess your strategy if the outcomes are unexpected—perhaps that seemingly brilliant concept doesn't end up being profitable after all. However, it is far preferable to do it now rather than after investing a lot of time and effort. A business advisor can help you understand some of the jargon used in business plans, which you can discover in information packs issued by banks to new enterprises or online.

Sometimes the outcomes can be unexpected—that seemingly brilliant concept doesn't end up being profitable after all—and you'll need to re-evaluate. But doing it now, before you devote all of your time and energy, is far better. Outline business plans can be found online or in the information packets that banks give to new enterprises, but an advisor can translate some of the business jargon for you.

ACCOUNTANT

As a self-employed individual or small business owner, you are not required to hire an accountant because you are capable of handling your own accounting needs and completing your own yearly tax returns. But in my opinion, unless you have a very low turnover, an accountant will probably pay for themselves by pointing out opportunities for you to claim tax deductions to lower your tax payment. There are certain allowances that are unique to your trade or profession, such as the ability to claim a portion of your household expenses if you use space in your home to run the business.

Even if you hire an accountant, it's a good idea to have a basic understanding of how to prepare and evaluate financial statements so that you may make informed inquiries about your company's financial performance and areas for improvement. In my experience, accountants rarely give information voluntarily and, unless you're lucky, only respond to questions directly posed to them.

A BANK MANAGER

It's wise to compare bank accounts before choosing one for your company. High-street banks provide free or

You might be able to negotiate a longer period than what is offered for low-cost financing to start-up companies for a predetermined time. Try to anticipate how many deposits and withdrawals you will make since you can incur bank fees if you do more than a specified number of transactions every month.

Consider whether this will work for you and your business before opening an internet or postal account because they do not provide counter service like those found in a branch. Such an account would not be appropriate, for instance, if you frequently get cash payments from domestic clients that you must deposit at a bank. If you are paid by check or bank transfer, that is OK.

It's important to keep in mind that bank managers aren't paid to provide you totally unbiased advice about how to run your company; rather, they work to increase profits for their employer. Search for a bank manager who responds to your idea and is excited about your company since you will find it easier to do business with them. However, bank employees frequently change jobs or are assigned to new responsibilities, so be ready for a change of personnel as well.

SOLICITOR

While it is not necessary to see a solicitor if you are simply starting your own business, I highly recommend it if you plan to form a partnership with one or more other persons. For more information on partnerships, please refer to the section above. Even though it's not required, you might wish to contact a lawyer if you've concluded that incorporation as a limited company is the best course of action. Request advice as usual.

AS A COACH OR MENTOR

If you believe you could accomplish more with the help of an objective outsider who can assess your opportunities and challenges, inspire you to take on challenges you might otherwise find too intimidating, and motivate you to do difficult things you might normally put off doing, hiring a coach may be beneficial. It's crucial that you get along well with your coach, so if you need to, talk to a few of them before choosing one. A mentor is someone who has more experience than you, has previously had some success, and is eager to lend you a helping hand. You can undoubtedly think of a professional in your field who you like and believe you might learn from. Invite them out for coffee and a talk to begin with, and then see how the relationship progresses.

ASSOCIATION OF PROFESSIONALS/INDUSTRIES

In terms of entry requirements, continuous training, licenses, certifications, complaints procedures, and other factors, depending on the business you choose, an organization may govern your operations. Once the conditions for admittance have been satisfied, you will typically need to pay an annual subscription to join, but this is frequently a wise investment. Professional associations frequently provide its members with insurance discounts and low-cost or free legal counsel. As a member, you may receive advantages including the right to use the association emblem on your marketing materials, which increases your reputation in the eyes of your clients, as well as chances to network with other professionals in the field.

Part 2

Making it Happen

4

HOW DO I CREATE MY PERFECT WORKSPACE?

Making your own workspace at home gives you the opportunity to do away with boring, grey cubicles and workstations and decorate it to reflect your hobbies and personality. This will make working there more motivating and inspiring.

The following topics are covered in this chapter:

1. Things to consider before creating a workstation at home or when enhancing an existing workspace.

2. Deciding whether to open your home to clients and other business partners.

3. Alternative locations if you don't want to have meetings in your house.

Organizing or upgrading your workspace

The following is a summary of the many things you should think about before picking where and how to set up your workspace. If you are planning a complete life makeover like some of the folks in this book, and moving home as well as out of the office, some of them, like geographic location, may not be things you can control, but they will be a significant factor. Both employees and self-employed people can benefit from each of the aforementioned characteristics.

CAN I WORK FROM HOME AND CARE FOR MY FAMILY IN THE PLACE I'VE SELECTED?

People have migrated away from cities and its amenities for a lot of years.

Regions and rural areas, where people regard daily life to be more tranquil and pleasant, are less stressful than those areas. If you have a home office, you may be considering relocating, especially if you have young children. Besides a few weeks spent in a summer home, have you and the other members of your family ever resided in a rural area? If there isn't a nearby print shop or post office, how will it influence your day-to-day activities? If every little errand requires a drive, can you complete your task properly and effectively? Many city inhabitants imagine living the good life in the country, which sometimes involves buying a home surrounded by expansive fields. However, they often give such plans serious consideration before moving.

Consider your typical day and, if you often buy your newspaper at the newsstand in the morning, buy a few groceries at the supermarket.

You most likely need these amenities to be reachable from your home office as well, so that you may leave for a quick walk around the block when you need a break and lunch.

IS THE SYSTEM SUFFICIENT?

In a similar vein, you should confirm that the local infrastructure allows you to work from home. We all need to have face-to-face meetings occasionally, despite the widespread and growing reliance on broadband, and adequate road, rail, and air linkages can allow you to arrive in good form. Additionally, given that gas is a considerable cost, traveling by airline or train can frequently be far cheaper than using your own vehicle.

WHICH LAWS APPLY WHEN CREATING A WORKSPACE AT HOME?

In spite of working from home, there are still regulations that must be followed, as we saw in Chapter 3. If you look into the following things before establishing your home office, you'll save yourself a lot of trouble and money.

Landlord Or Mortgage Lender

You should verify your title records to see if there are any restrictive covenants pertaining to commercial usage if you own your house and want to operate a business from it. Additionally, you must inform your mortgage provider of your intention to work from home.

Check your lease agreement if you rent your house because it might only be for residential usage. Landlords typically don't object if you work from their property.

rather than operating a business from home, but are likely to oppose to using the home for any purpose other than administrative work. You won't be able to have business guests at your house as a result.

Insurance

In order to avoid having your policies for buildings and contents insurance become invalid and not paying out if you make a claim, remember to inform your insurance provider that you will be working from home. The business will typically want to know if you plan to have a lot of visitors or if you'll be keeping expensive equipment and merchandise on the premises. If not, they might just change the wording of your insurance without adding any more premiums.

One of the first things you should think about while setting up at home, especially if you utilize pricey tools or supplies, is insurance.

Security and Health

Remember all those office rules concerning trip hazards like trailing cables, sticking-out drawers, and fraying carpets even if you work alone since you still have a responsibility to keep yourself safe. You should conduct a risk assessment of your operations if you have visitors to your home office or co-workers. This means you should identify all the hazards associated with doing the work you do and take actionable steps to mitigate them.

If you are an employee, your employer will generally request that you conduct your own risk assessment and make arrangements for Portable Appliance Testing (PAT) for your computer and any other electrical appliances you use. Every year, each appliance needs to be certified.

Planning Approval

Remember to confirm what permissions are required from your local authority before beginning work if building work is necessary to fit your new workstation in the house or out in the garden.

If you're operating a business from home rather than merely working from home, you should also confirm with the local government that you are authorized to do so in a residential neighbourhood, especially if the business will generate any noise, odours, or passing traffic. Remember that many businesses have been shut down as a result of complaints made to the council by irate neighbours. Don't assume that you can just proceed on the quiet. You must notify the environmental health division of your local authority if your business involves food preparation.

WHAT SHOULD I COMMUNICATE TO MY NEIGHBORS?

It's better to inform the neighbours about your plans now rather than risk having your workday disturbed if they become irate later. You may not be making any noise or having any other antisocial side effects, but it's still a good idea. However, they may also be happy that you will be around all day and therefore increase neighbourhood security. Neighbours are typically most angry when visitors use valuable parking places.

WHAT SIZES OF ROOM WILL I NEED?

You'll need space for at least a desk, chair, storage, and any other areas your work requires. You should also allow enough room so that you can open drawers, have easy access to outlets, replace the ink in your printer, and other things.

In order to avoid having to make significant adjustments again in a few months, it is a good idea to think positively when establishing a firm and to provide space for expansion (file storage, more equipment, etc.).

If you work for another person, it is certain that you will gather a lot of paper and other items that need to be stored. The place may need to be checked out by the employer.

which you intend to work, and they may refuse to let you work from home if they think your workspace and working environment are unsafe.

HOW DO I SET UP MY WORKSPACE?

Consider the space that is currently available in your home and garden and how you can modify it to utilize it as a home office when choosing where to place your desk, assuming that you are in the fortunate situation of having a choice.

Consider the real tasks you will be performing at work on a daily and irregular basis, not just the time you will spend sitting at a desk. That spare bedroom on the first floor might not be the best location if you need to store a lot of heavy materials or equipment or if your job includes transporting large objects—sofas and chairs, for example, if you upholster furniture. Your potential choices include:

- the kitchen or dining table
- a nook in the living room
- a landing or under the stairs
- a second bedroom

- the attic/loft o the garage
- an addition or separate garden room

DOES MY WORKSPACE NEED TO BE IN A DIFFERENT ROOM?

I keep reading in articles on working from home that having a door you can close to keep your home office separate from the rest of the house is crucial so you can work in peace and quiet, close it behind you when the working day is through, and forget about work is important. Although many people may view it as the ideal, the beauty of homeworking is that it may represent your personality as much you want it to, and we are all unique.

The issue with working while the family is present is that you might need to continuously putting your work away at supper or when you have company. You could use a screen to prevent staring at your workstation the entire evening or rearrange the furniture to create a separate working area to avoid this. Or you could spend your money on one of those furniture items that resembles a wardrobe but opens up to expose a desk and space for a computer and can be entirely closed up when you're done working.

CAN A HOME BE VALUED HIGHER IF IT HAS A WORKSPACE?

Make sure you are adding value and not making an eccentric, permanent modification that will suit you but turn off a potential buyer by taking into account the impact your improvements are likely to have on the value of your home. Many purchasers will appreciate a well-designed home office, and it could potentially increase the value of the property. Consult an estate agent before making any major alterations since they will be able to advise you on the best improvements to make to increase the charm and value of your home.

WHAT ABOUT THE HEATING AND LIGHTING?

The quality of your job will suffer if your home office isn't comfortable. You should have appropriate, adjustable heating and a source of fresh air, ideally a window you can gaze out of when in need of inspiration. Keep in mind that you can feel very cold sitting still at a computer for hours in the winter or very hot without any ventilation in the summer. Natural light, which is the nicest and most calming on the eyes, is also provided by windows. If artificial lighting is required, make sure it is even and doesn't reflect off your computer screen.

IS NEW FURNITURE REQUIRED FOR MY HOME?

Although it may be tempting to go on a shopping binge when setting up your workspace, it is not necessary to spend a lot of money, particularly if you are starting a business, you may already be on a tight budget. You might be able to use furniture you currently own, but keep in mind that you'll want to be comfortable and have a good back support while you're working. You shouldn't purchase office furniture without first giving it a try. Because you'll be using it for a long time, it needs to be comfy.

A decent middle ground would be to purchase used office furniture from a retailer who purchases surplus stock and cleans it up. In this way, you can feel like you're helping the environment while also getting well-designed items at a reasonable price. The Yellow Pages or the local newspaper both list outlets.

The quantity of furnishings and tools your business gives you will likely be proportional to the length of time you spend working remotely.

Desk

Your workstation should be large enough to fit your screen, keyboard, and speakers in addition to allowing you to write on an A4 pad and transfer documents about. Less eye fatigue results from a matte surface.

Chair

If you spend a lot of time at your desk, invest in a swivel chair with castors so you can easily turn around to reach items in your cabinet without having to push back a regular chair. A base with five spokes will be more stable than one with four.
Verify the chair's tilt and height adjustments and that your back is supported. If you can't comfortably lay your feet on the floor, use a footrest. If you have back issues, search for an ergonomic or kneeling chair. If they prevent you from rolling the chair beneath the desk, arm rests can be a hassle.

Storage

To keep documents and other items organized, you will need some type of storage. To avoid feeling demoralized by the prospect of all the work still to be done, I like to keep as much as possible hidden. Traditional workplace filing cabinets consume mountains of paper, and their deep drawers can conceal little pieces of technology. To adhere to an employer's confidentiality policy, you might need a shredder and lockable drawers.

HOW SHALL I SET UP MY WORKSPACE?

If you're fortunate enough to have a really spacious room for your new workstation, most people

The placement of your furniture and equipment is already constrained by variables in rooms, such as doors, windows, radiators, and electrical outlets. As opposed to a fully blank canvas, which might be confusing, this can actually be advantageous because it offers you a starting point around which to put everything. The only way to determine whether your workspace is practical and effective is to use it, so take your initial layout as a trial run and promise yourself that if it doesn't work well for you, you'll adjust it. The feeling that you made a mistake and must start over again is even more demoralizing than this.

IDEAS FOR SPACIOUS USE
Making the most of the space you have is important because home offices typically have limited space:

- You may roll a small pedestal cabinet on wheels neatly below a desk or use it as a tabletop for a printer.

- Put your printer or scanner on top of the filing cabinet because this area tends to collect clutter if it isn't used.

- You might want to use a laptop as your primary computer. It allows you vital movement while saving desk space.

- To conserve money, space, and electrical outlets, get multi-function devices that can copy, print, fax, and scan.

- To minimize space, mount your phone and desk lamp on the wall. Where there is no space for furniture, a low, wide shelf can store a printer.

- Ask a joiner to mould a piece of wood or a worktop to fit into a corner or an alcove that is awkwardly formed.

WHO FINANCES THE OPERATIONAL COSTS OF MY WORKSPACE?

You will be able to deduct a percentage of your home's operating expenses from your taxes if you are self-employed. But please with an accountant on this to make sure you won't be saddled with a capital gains tax bill from the government when you sell your residence.

Employers are likely to assume that any costs associated with working from home will be compensated by the money you save on travel, so they might be reluctant to pay for the heating and lighting of your home office.

WHERE DOES THE IT SIDE OF THINGS STAND?

Sockets:

Calculate how many electrical outlets you'll need for your computer, printer, scanner, fax, etc. and add a few more for unforeseen needs. Instead of overtaxing the system by plugging numerous appliances into an adaptor, install more sockets if necessary. Consider placing sockets at desk level rather than just above the skirting board if you are starting from scratch so you can easily reach them.

Phone

In order to utilize the phone for internet, you might need to install at least one additional phone socket, thus it might be a good idea to think about getting separate phone lines for your home and company. The benefit of having two lines is that you always know how to respond when the phone rings—you can say hello or provide a formal professional response. You may also want to prevent the kids from answering the business line. Regarding preserving a professional image, see Chapter 6 as well.

Computer

Your profession will determine whether you use a Mac or PC, and whether you continue with a laptop. The Health and Safety Executive (HSE) advises that when using a computer, your forearms should be nearly horizontal and your eyes should be at eye level with the top of the screen. Get up frequently to give your body and eyes a rest, and use a relaxed arm and straight wrist to operate the mouse.

The HSE suggests that short breaks should be taken frequently rather than longer ones less frequently. For instance, instead of 20 minutes every two hours, they advise a five-to-ten-minute break every hour.

There may be guidelines set forth by your employer regarding whether you may use their equipment for personal use or permit use by others. There is a warning story about a child using his mother's computer while she is doing her homework in Chapter 8.

Broadband

Nearly everyone in the UK now has access to broadband, but it's still a good idea to double-check your options and the speed. You can network multiple computers together using either hardwired connections or wireless ones, while wireless networks have received unfavourable press due to potential health risks.

You will lose a lot of bandwidth if someone else is working with you or if your kids are playing computer games concurrently with your job. If the bandwidth is insufficient to support both activities, think about getting two internet connections. For use at home or at work, broadband is available. Although using a home connection is less expensive, more individuals share the bandwidth. Check to see if there are any download restrictions before signing up since if your kids are downloading games and videos, your allotment may be depleted very quickly.

Technology Assistance

Finding a capable and affordable computer engineer right away will be more advantageous than waiting until anything goes wrong. What about archiving your work? In the event of an emergency, such as a fire, IT professionals advise you to retain a backup off-site. Even if you never need to use them, having plans in place to handle such events reduces your stress levels, so have a look at Chapter 9 as well.

Save cash while protecting the environment.

Additional suggestions for reducing family and business expenses while also helping the environment are provided below:
When you leave your desk, turn off the light. If your office equipment has a stand-by feature, turn it off and unplug it at night to avoid wasting money on energy.

- When you need a break, switch off your monitor.

- Print on both sides of the page if you can, and save the mistakes for scrap.

- Look for the Print This Page button when printing content from the internet, or cut and paste just the necessary data into a Word document.

- Use the Print in Grayscale/Black Cartridge Only and Fast draft options wherever applicable, and decrease font size and margins to fit more text on a page. (You can find this using the print properties button on your computer's print window.)

- Recycle your shredded paper or place it in the compost container.

- Recycle plastic bottles, paper, cardboard, printer ink, cell phones, and electronics.

- When utilizing a brand-new folder, attach a white label to it and jot down the subject in pencil. Rub out the name once the job is finished, then start over.

- Boil just a cup or mugful of water for your coffee, not the entire kettle.

- Attach a thermostatic valve to the radiator in your office so you may control the heating independently of the rest of the house.

- Send Christmas e-cards. Two years ago, we did it with a lot of hesitation, and the reaction from clients and colleagues was overwhelmingly favourable. Spend less on cards and postage and donate the money to your favourite charity; it soon adds up.

DECORATION

The fun part now is making your workstation a pleasant place to be since the paperwork and physical necessities are all taken care of. Even so, keep in mind the impression it can provide if you ever have visitors. It doesn't even need to look like an office.

You can decorate the walls with your favourite paint colours and patterns or wall coverings, and hang the artwork, posters, and images that motivate and inspire you. It's a good idea to put mementos of your accomplishments and successes on display, such as credentials, diplomas, prizes, and letters of gratitude. Your confidence will increase as you observe these. You will be motivated to work harder when you see pictures of your family since they will serve as a reminder of why you are doing it. Purchase colourful files instead of the drab, institutional ones that are packaged and make everything appear so monotonous.

Some people get inspiration from putting a "dream board" above their workstation, which is a notice board where you can post photographs of the things you wish to accomplish, such as a house, a car, a vacation spot, professional recognition, a significant contract, etc. The idea is that by always being in your thoughts, the images serve as a reminder to press on when times are difficult and will also help you attract the conditions and people you need to realize your goals. It must be worthwhile to try.

The addition of plants to your workspace is beneficial. They not only provide the environment a burst of colour and vibrancy, but they also remove airborne pollutants, boost the amount of oxygen and negatively charged ions in the air, which reduces the harmful health impacts of electronic devices. Philodendrons, rubber plants, and peace lilies are all excellent for this.

DO I NEED TO KEEP MY WORKPLACE PRIVACY?

Now that your home office is organized, you have complete control over who enters and when. The benefits and drawbacks of having visitors at your workspace are discussed in the next section. In Chapter 8, we discuss creating healthy boundaries between work and home, including rules for kids. Here is an illustration of how the extended family might profit from working from home in the interim:

Should I open my office to visitors?

When you work from home for another person, you probably follow a set of rules on who is allowed to visit you at home — co-workers are typically okay — and who is not — typically clients and associates who are affiliated with other organizations. Thus, you avoid having to decide who, if anyone, should visit a self-employed person at home, a decision that is frequently required.

ADVANTAGES OF HOLDING MEETINGS AT HOME

- It could be difficult to come up with other places to meet people if you spend all or a large portion of your time working from home.
- It would be inconvenient to carry your materials, books, records, and other items outside of your home.
- You are literally in "home turf" and would feel uncomfortable elsewhere.
- Your visitor might love the casual atmosphere and getting to know your home and family. It might prompt them to do business with you.

DISADVANTAGES OF HAVING MEETINGS AT HOME

- Even if you run your business from your kitchen table very effectively, how will that come across to clients or suppliers? Will it give you a less professional and more amateurish appearance?

- Both your business and your entire house and lifestyle will be investigated.
  If you only have an upstairs bathroom and guests must go through the entire home to access it, you will need to make sure the house is always clean and neat before having guests.

- How will your family gatherings affect the other members? It's possible that your partner or kids won't enjoy having to be quiet or out of sight for the duration.

- You might be nervous the entire meeting in case family members or an unexpected caller interrupt you, or you might be unclear about how to conduct a business meeting in a setting where you usually only host family and friends.

- When the line between a professional and personal encounter is blurred, your customer might not know how to act. They can feel under pressure to praise your furnishings or your kids, and unsure of how to begin and end the conversation.

- Because of the amount of intimacy required to enter someone's house, some people may feel under pressure to work with you instead of choosing to do so.

Your decision regarding whether or not to hold all or parts of your meetings at home will be influenced by your family situation, your residence, the nature of your job, and the adaptability of your business partners. Try one of the below-listed alternatives, or consider about investing in the ultimate solution—a fully independent workplace with a separate entrance—so that guests never have to enter your home.

A Substitute for Home Meetings

There are some workarounds if you decide that your situation does not permit having business guests in your home office.

VISIT THEM

Dealing with companies that operate out of their own location allows you to prevent any problems from ever occurring by constantly recommending a visit. The majority of people are too busy to even notice that you always visit them; they'll just be relieved not to have to travel to see you. Perhaps they won't even be aware that you work from home.

If a private individual is receptive, visiting them at home might be most convenient. Make sure you take reasonable precautions to safeguard your safety if you don't know them well.

CAFÉ SHOPS ET AL

A coffee shop or hotel lobby may be the appropriate location, depending on the circumstance and whether your conversation is confidential. However, you should carefully consider the formality, privacy, and noise levels as well as how long you can reasonably expect to be there before making your decision. Trying to speak above the sound of clattering dishes is exhausting and unprofessional, and conversing with a stranger in a public area while other customers listen in is humiliating and off-putting.

Avoid any unpleasant connotations of a "date" that can make the meeting uncomfortable for you both if you are meeting someone of the opposing sex. Put your commercial relationship at danger.

JOB CENTRE

If you are a business looking to hire through your local Jobcentre, they might be able to provide you with a free interview space. For further information, get in touch with your local office as availability varies by Jobcentre size.

A ROOM TO RENT

Cosmetology / Alternative Medicine Clinic

Your neighbourhood salon or complementary health centre might have rooms available to rent for the day or a half-day if you are a therapist or counsellor of some kind. By being on the high street and being a part of their promotion, you will raise your profile.

Hotel, Restaurant, Cafe, And Pub Rooms

Cafes, restaurants, and bars frequently have private rooms available to rent for an hour or half-day if you need to conduct a meeting or interview a large number of individuals. Others may give it for free as long as you purchase refreshments, while some may charge for using the space.

Public Spaces

Today's village and community halls are frequently of a high calibre and willing to rent out space in order to generate income.

Units for company start-up and incubation

Low-cost units for new firms in particular industries may be offered by your local government and university.

Office Space with Services

You can rent serviced office space, paying to use a facility, in numerous towns and cities to reserve a desk, office, or conference room for a certain period of time, as well as the usage of services like printing, copying, and phone calls.

Work-hubs

In some parts of the country, business support organizations, local governments, and other interested parties are collaborating to raise money for the construction of so-called "work hubs" for small local home-based businesses, which will aid them in overcoming the kinds of difficulties we discuss in this book. Work hubs offer an affordable setting for client meetings on neutral ground or merely to get out of the house, experience a fascinating new atmosphere, and network with other companies and potential business partners. If your business is growing and you want to move it outside of your home, they are the perfect next step due to their cost. Work hubs are also being used as a hub for the distribution of business advice that would otherwise be inaccessible to firms hidden away at home.

THE FUTURE OF HOMEWORKING: LIVE/WORK UNITS?

Live/work properties are a relatively new idea that is gaining ground in acceptance. Unlike homes where a spare room has been installed as a home office or turned into one, live/work dwellings are built from the ground up to allow both living and working space. The space used for business purposes tends to take up more room in live/work units, which may be able to support additional workers and business expansion.

When land use has historically been divided into home and commercial use, a number of challenges with the novel idea of live/work properties occur, including acquiring planning approval to build them. Live/work properties also pose a threat to conventional financial norms because some lenders are hesitant to issue mortgages for such properties and limit the amount of space that may be used for commercial purposes. The obligations of a live/work unit owner with relation to council tax, capital gains tax, and VAT are still far from clear-cut at the time of writing. If only government employees could be as resourceful and flexible as homeworkers.

5

CAN I BE PRODUCTIVE AT HOME?

Working with others automatically enlists you in a dynamic system that calls for your participation and puts pressure on you to perform. It makes sense that many people worry that, while working from home and being free from the politics of the workplace and many interruptions, they may find it challenging to accomplish anything as there is no outside motivation to finish their work.

You will learn the following in this chapter:

1.   That people who work from home can be significantly more productive
        than people who work in an office.
2.   Create your own, most effective working from home method.
3.   Establish a schedule for your day to help you stay focused.
4.   Learn how to prevent time wasters by becoming aware of them.
5.   Recognize the causes of your procrastination and the solutions you can use.

Are you productive or sluggish, miserable, and fat?

According to a study done by the Australian publication Home Beautiful in the early part of 2007, many of its readers were concerned that working from home would lead to them becoming "fat, miserable, and lazy." A fifth of those surveyed said being alone would be demoralizing, while a third of respondents said they would spend the day eating and watching television.

Away from the numerous distractions of the traditional workplace, however, almost half of respondents thought they would be more productive, and this is exactly what BT has discovered; their home workers are on average 20% more productive than their office-based colleagues. Even this great number is negligible in comparison to the SusTel (Sustainable Teleworking) project findings from the UK Centre for Economic and Environmental Development, which were released in 2004. The research looked into the effects of working from home on the economy, the environment, and society in five European nations, including the UK.

Higher productivity was one of the benefits of homeworking that was most frequently noted by the people I spoke with during my research for this book, so I know this to be the case. In fact, many people who work from home discover that, far from being inefficient, their biggest issue is avoiding becoming overly engrossed in their work and working far more hours than their office-based colleagues. When work is done at the dining room table or in the study, it is quite simple to stay working until there is little time left for personal or family activities, and then to return after dinner or on weekends to check emails and voicemails.

Higher productivity was one of the advantages of homeworking that was most frequently stated by the people I met with during my research for this book, so I can say with certainty that they believe this to be the case. In fact, a lot of people who work from home discover that, far from being unproductive, their biggest issue is avoiding being overly engrossed in their work and working far longer hours than their co-workers who work in offices. It's quite simple to stay working until there is very little time left for personal and family interests when work is done at the dining room table or in the study, and then to return there after dinner or on weekends to check emails and voicemails.

Employee performance has historically been evaluated more on the number of hours spent in the office than on the volume of work completed. We've all met those people who never do a thing but manage to persuade management that they are functioning well. In a 2005 poll by America Online and Salary.com, American workers acknowledged squandering more than two hours of work time each day on the internet, chit-chatting with co-workers, and taking care of personal business.
Therefore, high levels of productivity cannot be guaranteed by simply being present.

Identifying your most effective working from home habits

In Chapter 2, I made the argument that knowing your personality and how you will probably react to the difficulties of working from home will offer you the best chance of succeeding in the endeavour. You will also spend your time more effectively if you are aware of seemingly unimportant personal peculiarities, such as the types of work you enjoy doing the most, the attire that makes you feel both professional and comfortable, and the time of day when you are most focused and productive. Asking yourself the following questions will help you to more objectively reflect on your habits. It could be beneficial to record your responses in a notepad and keep adding to it when you have more to say. It could take some time for you to fully develop a vision of your ideal working pattern. These are the inquiries.

WHICH TIME OF DAY ARE YOU MOST EFFECTIVE?

Do you often start the day off with a burst of energy or do you require multiple cups of coffee to ease you into the day, only to find your groove by mid-morning? You might be one of those persons who doesn't start being creative until the day's distractions have passed. Or are you required to be as productive as you can be while the kids are at day care? Was the time of day an influence in a recent moment when you were happy with your work?

WHAT WILL YOU BE WEARING?

Working from home has several freeing benefits, like the freedom from having to follow a dress code and the potential financial savings from not having to purchase and dry-clean "business attire." Theoretically, you may now spend the entire day lounging about in your pyjamas and dressing gown, but I've never encountered a homeworker who did, possibly because they quickly realize that clothes have a significant impact on your mood and, thus, your productivity. Financial advisor Neil conducts some of his business from home. In order to get into a professional frame of mind, he discovers that he needs to put on his suit, exactly as he would if he were going to the office or to see a client. Don't undervalue the power of clothing; pay attention to how different looks affect you. feel. Being a homeworker may require you to re-evaluate your wardrobe and even purchase some new clothes.

WHAT KIND OF WORKING MODE DO YOU PREFER?

Do you require as much silence as possible to focus, or do you like the background noise of the radio or a CD? A writer named Robin works silently at first, but when he senses his pace slipping, he cranks on some upbeat music to get him going again. Note down your own preferences. Do you fall into the category of those who find it impossible to function while conversations or when music has lyrics? Alternatively, perhaps you simply want a soft radio to keep you company?

Keep in mind that your preferences could alter over time or in response to certain activities. Liam used earplugs to help him when he began working from home as a freelance writer.

to "get in the zone." He eventually started utilizing the earplugs and classical music at the same time. He doesn't truly comprehend the habit; he only knows that it benefits him.

WHAT POSITIONS COME NATURALLY TO YOU?

American motivational speaker Brian Tracy claims that in order to be most effective, you should "eat that frog" first thing in the morning! In other words, the remainder of the day will be simple if you can immediately do the task that bothers you the most. Which tasks do you keep putting off? Make a list of your tasks in the opposite direction from the order you like. If you can train yourself to complete the tasks at the top of your list first and without too much pain, you'll have the remainder of the day to enjoy the remaining tasks. Use your list to help you arrange your day, which is something we'll discuss later in the chapter.

WHAT DO YOU REALLY DO WITH YOUR TIME?

It is simple to fool yourself into thinking you are working hard when in reality you are wasting a lot of time checking emails, browsing the internet, preparing snacks and drinks, or conversing about things unrelated to work.
Consider creating a chart that breaks your day into quarter-hour segments, much to how lawyers do it to determine how much to charge clients. Record your progress on the chart devoted each period of time. Then, check back in a week or so to see how you are actually spending your time. How much time you waste on useless hobbies can astound you. If so, continue on to the chapters regarding time management and procrastination further in this one. In Chapter 2, Kevin describes how he realized he was squandering time and made changes to his routines to become more effective.

SEE TO IT THAT YOU RECOGNIZE AND CELEBRATE YOUR SUCCESSES.

There are undoubtedly times when you feel like there aren't enough hours in the day. Stay up with all the developments in your industry or job by running nonstop.

When you accomplish anything, it's simple to barely recognize it before moving on to the next goal or task, especially if no one is present to share in your joy. Make a point of pausing to give yourself a pat on the back, perhaps call someone to express your gratitude, and treat yourself to lunch out or a small gift. Celebrating in this way keeps your enthusiasm and self-assurance high and provides you something to look forward to when you're having trouble finishing a task.

Establishing A Daily Schedule and Maintaining Concentration

You may create a functional schedule for your day after you are aware of what motivates you and what your preferences are. Start with factors like the school run and structure your day around them as commitments connected to children or other responsibilities may affect how you organize your day.

KEEPING A DIARY

A diary, whether it be a classic book and pen, an application on your computer, or a handheld device, is necessary if you do your homework at home. You may avoid scheduling conflicts by entering all of your domestic and professional commitments into your calendar as soon as you make them. If you're just starting off working from home, you might want to specify breaks and your expected completion time.

To ensure that you are making progress toward your objective, it is a good idea to write down deadlines and break the work involved into manageable sections with their own dates.

COMPLETING HOUSEWORK

I find that it's better to neglect everything but the shortest and most basic tasks, just as you probably won't have time to complete any housework before leaving home to commute to work.

if your workplace is at home, household chores. Once you get cleaning and organizing, it's simple to get sucked into an hour or two of work. Even though it is a special form of labour and makes you feel good, it doesn't actually pay you any money.

It might be expected of you to handle the majority of the housework if you work from home and your partner commutes to the office. For now, just remember that the first thing in the morning might be a good time to disregard the domestic duties. We look at setting limits in Chapter 8.

RELOCATING TO WORK FROM HOME

To make the shift from night-time activities and start the workday smoothly, it is essential to have some sort of schedule. When you commute to work from home, your thinking can shift from personal to professional worries. This is especially true if you work from home. You'll need to devise an alternative strategy if your employment is done from home.

Before going back home and starting their jobs, I've heard of folks getting up, dressing nicely, and going outside to walk around the block. An avid cyclist was known to a buddy who would ride in the morning and then begin working after taking a shower. Investigate what signals to you that it's time to enter business mode on your own to see what works. Due to my varied obligations and the fact that I grow bored when the same thing happens every day, my own routine has changed frequently throughout the years and will undoubtedly do so again. If yours becomes too routine, change it; you'll feel more energetic.

BEGINNING YOUR DAY

You're sitting at your desk or workbench, but perhaps you're still not feeling like working. These actions could be beneficial.

- Always check your calendar first thing in the morning to avoid missing appointments or early phone calls. It's good to organize your day now, keeping in mind when you'll need to leave work to get ready for a meeting or drive to pick up the kids. (For advice on keeping track of time, see Chapter 2, "How Do You Keep Time?").

- Start your day by visiting any websites you have come across in articles from magazines and newspapers or in advertising. They may have to do with your job or pleasure. Visit your preferred newspaper's website, perhaps. Checking for new messages in your inbox or on the forums is a good idea if you are a member of an online network (see Chapter 7).

- Online bank account checks for your personal or corporate accounts. There is no excuse, my business advisor used to say, for not always knowing exactly how much money is in your account. It's a good idea to search frequently so that you won't be caught off guard by a sizable forthcoming commitment since the majority of us undoubtedly don't fulfil these demanding standards. Not to mention the motivation your existing balance might offer, whether it is reassuringly big or uncomfortably skinny.

- Observe emails next. When Nikki's internet was down for a few weeks and her publishing company couldn't check their email first thing in the morning, she noticed the difference: It was challenging to start underway. Day begins with emails. They frequently establish the tone for the day and direct my activities and priority-setting.

- Call someone right now. Speaking with others may help you stay motivated and may give you some deadlines or help you prioritize your task.

ESTABLISHING BREAK TIMES

Before you even begin working, you might wish to schedule breaks are frequently established at work and rigorously followed. Put your break times in the calendar along with your meetings and appointments. You might set your phone or an alarm clock to ring and remind you to take a break if you are an in-time person (see Chapter 2) and frequently lose track of time. It is tempting to believe you can keep working despite becoming less and less productive.

Remember that the human brain can only focus for around 20 minutes at a time. I've discovered that the maximum amount of time I can work without losing steam is two hours.

EXPLORING THE FRESH AIR

Even if it's just to run down the street for a newspaper, I find that leaving the house at least once a day is necessary. Use the flexibility you have; your office-bound buddies are so envious of you. You are now in a situation where you may mix work and pleasure. After a meeting, go out to lunch, visit a friend, or go for a stroll in the park.

After lunch, most of us aren't particularly productive, so this is a good time to go for a stroll to get some fresh air and a new perspective. It's all too simple to forget that there is an entire universe taking place outside your workroom door. Make it a point to engage in conversation with others while you are out and about. We will discuss how to create and sustain support networks in Chapter 7. Without a sense of connection to a broader system, you risk coming to a halt.

TAKING NAP

Knowing that many people feel bad about wasting time, they avoid taking naps during the day. In fact, I link taking naps with working hard because I frequently had to leave the house early in the morning to check on the cleanliness of the office when I managed my cleaning business. I took an afternoon break after finishing my organization and administration tasks before going out in the evening to visit my cleaners while they were at work. A midday nap was necessary for me occasionally since I was physically exhausted. I don't work out as much these days, but I still think that taking a nap might help my brain feel refreshed. By turning my busy conscious mind off, it allows my unconscious mind to have a chance to come up with a thought. I think that many of us may really be negatively impacted by the work ethic we ingrained from our parents. We are just unable to work continuously because we require downtime to properly process and assimilate new information before applying it.

EATING

What about the worry that people who participated in the Australian magazine survey on homeworking voiced about being "fat, miserable, and lazy"? (See this chapter's introduction.) When work is not going well, it is so simple to get up, make a cup of coffee, a few biscuits, and maybe even some of the pie that was left over from the previous evening.

When working from home, Chapter 8 discusses how to maintain your health and weight. Have an attractive fruit bowl full of healthy snacks to keep your energy up throughout the day. Pumpkin seeds and nuts both include vitamin E, which is connected to improved memory, and will provide you the daily necessary amount of zinc, which supports your brain function and memory.

GETTING WEARY

Recognizing the signs that you need a break or to switch to something else for a bit when you are growing bored of a task is helpful. The word count button is a tell-tale sign that I need to stop writing when I run out of ideas, I've discovered when writing. I can return later with fresher thinking if I go off and read or clean the home.

SUM UP YOUR DAY

When you are organizing your daily routine, you might want to establish a finishing time in advance, perhaps at or near the time that your co-workers who work from home are logging off and entering the lines of commuters. Their return signifies the conclusion of the workday, but you might require a similar pattern to your morning one—perhaps another bike ride or dog walk—to emphasize that domestic matters can now take control. You can definitely help yourself to switch off from work-related thoughts by leaving the house and placing some physical distance between you and your tools or the computer.

BEING EFFICIENT WITH YOUR TIME

There is a vast quantity of information available, including books, the internet, and training programs, on the topic of time management, which has recently become one of the hottest topics. The truth is, though, that you are completely incapable of managing time. You may control yourself by setting priorities for the demands on your time. This is the subject of a well-known tale. Depending on where you read it, the specifics change, but the fundamental idea stays the same.

THE BEST-PAID TIME MANAGEMENT TIP EVER?

Charles Schwab oversaw Bethlehem Steel in the 1930s, which was the biggest independent steel manufacturer in the country at the time. He sought advice from renowned management guru Ivy Lee on how to boost organizational effectiveness. Lee offered the following piece of advice:

1.   Make a list of all the tasks you need to complete tomorrow and rank the top
       five in terms of importance.

2.   As soon as you get to work tomorrow morning, begin working on the first
       thing and don't stop until it is finished, or as finished as you are able to make
       it.

3.   Next, begin work on the next item. Only take care of additional tasks during
       the day if they are more crucial than the one you are currently working on. If
       not, put them in order of importance on your list.

4.   Create a new list of the next five tasks once you have completed the first five as far as you can. If you are unable to complete everything on the list, at least the most crucial tasks will be finished, so it won't be a problem.

ELIMINATING TIME WASTERS

Avoid doing what Americans refer to as "busy work," which are tasks that give the impression that you are progressing with your work but actually do nothing. Procrastination can quickly take over these activities. And other tasks will gladly consume all the time you can offer them while producing very little. The ones to be on the lookout for are these.

HOW TO WORK WITH EMAILS

You can save time by establishing some straightforward rules for the use and processing of emails. My favorited email advice is as follows:

- Only download your emails twice or three times per day. The middle of the morning and the middle of the afternoon are good times since it gives people time to send you things in the morning and provides you time to react before the end of the day. Respond right away. It's simple to say, "I'll take care of that later," and then to forget.

- Delete as many emails as you can right away, or place them in labelled folders for later use. Then, the emails in your inbox will only be those that need a response or that require action. If you have to scroll down to read the emails in your inbox, out of sight can all too quickly become out of mind.

- Be explicit when composing subject lines, and try to include details that will make it simple for recipients to identify the email, such as names, dates, and times. Unique subject headers can save you from having to spend time scrolling through a big list of emails with generic subject lines like "Invoice" or "Meeting" when you need to quickly locate a specific email.

- Prepare common responses to frequent inquiries and save the templates in your Draft folder. However, make sure to customize each response before sending it out. If you have spent time and thought crafting a nice message, you don't want to undermine its impact by making the reader aware that it is a conventional draft.

- While phone conversations are sometimes quicker and easier than emails for keeping in touch, they are still sometimes necessary, such as when you need to get in touch with a group of people to make changes to plans. Emails may be fantastic for keeping in touch. Never take an email for granted that it has been read by the intended recipient or that the reply hasn't also gone astray.

- Even when there is a problem to fix, it can be tempting to use email as a substitute for verbal communication. However, this is precisely the time when you should speak with them. Emails might easily have the wrong tone and intention, which could lead to an escalation of the situation. To catch typing errors and look for potential misinterpretations, always read emails again before hitting the Send key. While you are aware of what was on your mind when you penned it, the reader may have a whole different interpretation. In order to draft an email and return to it later, try to provide enough time if the topic is critical. You might notice certain adjustments that need to be made when viewing things with fresh eyes.

- This last issue, which seems so basic but which I occasionally encounter, is EMAILS TYPED IN

CAPITALS. Though it sounds hectoring and leaves a terrible impression, it is likely that the sender believes the contents to be significant.

DIRECTING MEETINGS

Working from home has its benefits, one of which is not having to go to as many meetings as you were required to at work. However, there are instances when face-to-face meetings are still the most effective means of communication.

Don't allow anyone to sit down during meetings, a very successful businessman once shared with me. What can you do to speed up the process if not remove the chairs from the room? I presume he was joking, despite how badly he may have wanted to. I've had success with these recommendations:

- The worst times for focus are late afternoon and right after lunch, so try to avoid them if you can.

- Send out an agenda so that everyone is aware of it at least one day in advance. Additionally, decide in advance who will take notes and write the minutes (someone who can understand the essential issues and write them up succinctly) and who will serve as the chairman (someone who is tactful but forceful and can stop people from wandering off on a tangent).

- Include a finish time in addition to the start time. Start the meeting on time, check the time frequently to stay on schedule, and wrap it up before the deadline. To avoid running over time, avoid interrupting the action to summarize for latecomers. To ensure that everyone is aware of what needs to be accomplished, summarize the action items at the conclusion.

- Do you ever attend meetings and question why you are expected to be there? Make your excuses and request to receive the minutes if you don't feel obligated to attend if you have nothing to add and nothing to learn.

UTILIZING A PHONE

A significant time waster is talking on the phone. My own pet peeve is folks that ramble on and on, keep saying the same thing, and don't listen when you try to end the conversation. Although there isn't much you can do about them, you can monitor your personal phone use. These are my guidelines for avoiding having calls consume my day.

- Only activate your phone when you intend to use it. The idea that everyone should be accessible all the time is something I vehemently disagree with. I think it's needless and obtrusive. I believe that my cell phone is for my convenience and no one else's.

- Don't be afraid to turn on the answering machine if you need to focus on a task (or take a nap!) People are used to leaving messages, so there is no expectation that you will always be immediately accessible. Just be sure to respond as soon as possible to your messages and don't forget to call back right away.

- Check that you have all the necessary information before calling. If you interrupt someone while speaking, it's embarrassing for both of you. When you call, avoid having apparent information like account numbers. Also, try to keep paper and a pen close by your phone because the person you want to impress is always the one who notices when you don't have them.

- Do you have the proper attitude to make this particular call? Your tone of voice reveals your mood, which the person you are speaking to will pick up on. It can be best to postpone till you are feeling better if you are feeling off or must make a sales call but don't feel up to it. However, avoid letting it led to procrastination. If you have trouble making calls, practice will make it easier.

- Be careful not to linger in conversation after your business question has been answered. By doing this, time can seemingly vanish.

MANAGEMENT PAPER

I can recall watching a movie about the "paperless office" in the 1970s when I was still in school. A movie was also made about how much leisure time we will all have due to the advancements in technology. These two, like so many other future prophecies, have proven to be false, and paper continues to flood unabatedly into our lives. If we don't take care of it right away, it can overwhelm us. Here is how to handle it.

o Handle mail as soon as it comes in. There are many things that may be thrown away or recycled right away, but in these times of identity theft, never forget to shred anything that contains personal information. Be brutal. Be mindful that if you are tempted to save something to "read later," it will probably never get read and will instead just build up on your desk in an unending, gloomy mound. Articles are soon out of date since information is now so easily accessible and changes so regularly. If you do require that information in the future, you'll probably need to double-check the facts nevertheless.

o If you are certain that you will need a piece of paper in the future, store it away. However, create a note in your calendar to clear your files at least once a year, around the time of tax season. When six years have passed, you can discard a year's worth of tax and company records, so now is a good time to start. I'm always astounded by how much things I've carefully stored and then entirely forgotten about when I go through my annual session on the shredder.

o Get a red pen if you discover that you frequently pick things up and set them down to "sort out later." Put a red dot in the corner each time you glance at the page. Hopefully, the abundance of red dots will motivate you to handle it and get it out of the way!

HOW TO STOP PROCRASTINATING AND WHAT YOU CAN DO

This is the major one for those who do their homework, isn't it? We all put things off, in my opinion. You postpone doing something that you know you should do eventually but could do right away. You put it off in an effort to make your life more enjoyable, but you frequently wind up making yourself feel pressured and guilty in the process. You can put off doing things in a variety of ways, some of which may even appear to be beneficial. Try to identify any of them.

- You put off starting the assignment by conducting additional study and accumulating information. You persuade yourself that this background information is important, but in reality, you are merely delaying the bad situation.

- You begin to clean and organize your immediate environment with an obsession that goes well beyond what is necessary. Before beginning that job, make sure you have all the necessary tools, furnishings, technology, books, etc.

- All of a sudden, other tasks take precedence, such as cleaning the kitchen floor, cleaning the oven, and ironing. It's all worthwhile work, but you know deep down that it's not moving you any closer to finishing the dreadful chore.

THEREFORE, WHY DO WE PROCRASTINATE?

Things might be delayed for a variety of reasons. The simplest explanation is that you dislike your job or don't fully grasp what is expected of you. If that's the case, you can fix it by doing something else, for instance, which is a really simple and practical action to take! It truly pays to focus on your abilities, which are what generate the revenue, and hire someone else to handle the tasks you detest but never get around to. This is especially true when you own your own firm. One excellent example is handling the books, but you can also delegate tasks like handling letters, pursuing unpaid invoices, and making sales calls to others.

It might be helpful to consider whether any of these are appropriate as there are sometimes more subtle factors that prevent advancement. You can begin to overcome them by simply recognizing them.

- It's possible that the sheer amount of work you have to complete has you feeling overwhelmed, and the anxiety prevents you from concentrating on starting.

- I've never been very good at this kind of stuff, so I'm scared I'll fail. What if I mess it up and make a fool of myself? Or perhaps you truly worry about failing: "What will happen if I succeed in this? Will I still be popular? What more might I be required to do?

- You struggle with perfectionism or having unattainable expectations. Before beginning to write on a subject, you might wish to read everything you can discover on it and keep looking for new information.

- You might be expecting your first attempts to appear like the completed product and become discouraged when they don't.

PROCRASTINATION CONTROL

Do not wait until the situation is hopeless and you are in a sad state to begin. Any of the aforementioned reasons for delaying should be easier for you to handle if you follow the advice below.

- You know that awful sinking sensation you get when, against yourself, the thought of a task you've put off for a while crosses your mind? Sometimes it can be a relief to really get started. To make it more pleasant, try saying to yourself, "Today I will do that thing and it will be a pleasure since then I won't have it at the back of my mind any more."

- Having a good old clear out might be a technique to jump-start the brain, as long as cleaning and organizing your workspace isn't one of your ways of delaying. Making room for fresh ideas to enter your mind can magically create space in your real environment.

- Keep in mind that the initial phase is the most challenging. If you can simply get moving, you will start to gather momentum. As you move forward, the momentum will only increase, carrying you along almost unconsciously.

- Divide the task into a number of manageable, little parts. After completing the first task, reward yourself with brewing a cup of coffee or reading the newspaper. If you keep doing this in short bursts, the magical momentum may begin to build.

- Or you could begin with the task you find the simplest or like the most. It might not be the best location to start, but if it gets you motivated, you can add it later.

- It can be challenging to begin writing a report or other piece of writing since you already see the finished product in your mind's eye. Write down all the concepts you identify with the subject during a brainstorming session. You can start to see how to develop your argument by grouping the ideas into categories. You can now focus on communicating your thoughts because the difficult work is finished.

- If you're feeling overwhelmed, heed the 1930s counsel of Ivy Lee (Making the most of your time, page 88). Sit down with a piece of paper and take a deep breath before listing all of your tasks in order of priority. Start with the most crucial task first, and continue working on it until you've completed it or done everything you can then move on to the next most crucial task, etc.

6

WHAT ABOUT MY PROFESSIONAL IMAGE?

It doesn't matter whether you operate primarily from home and are therefore invisible to the outside world; maintaining a professional appearance and demeanour is still imperative.

This chapter, which is followed by parts geared first to the demands of people in employment and then those of those running home enterprises, addresses three topics that are essential for all homeworkers, whether they are employed or working for themselves:

1.   The necessity to retain secrecy in written and verbal communications in the
        comfortable setting of your own home.

2.   Techniques for regularly offering exceptional customer service that will make
        you in high demand (while keeping in mind that you can be "serving" colleagues rather than paying clients).

3.   How to conduct yourself such that others would respect and believe you to be professional in everything you do.

4.   Advice for working from home while staying on top of the game even if you
        don't see your co-workers every day.

5.   Suggestions for self-employed people on how to present a consistent brand to everyone you interact with.

The significance of confidentiality

It can be easy to adopt an overly casual attitude concerning the secrecy of the material you're dealing with when working in your home office, away from the prying eyes of co-workers and guests. I'm not arguing that your relatives or guests would use the information for questionable purposes, but you owe your clients and co-workers a high standard of caution. Failure to do so could cost you your job or your reputation, both of which are difficult to recover from. Keep your communications private in the following ways.

- Provide yourself with a private area where you may examine documents and make phone calls without being seen or overheard. This is quite beneficial.

- Keep computer passwords hidden from other family members and store documents away in a file cabinet when you are done using them. (Chapter 8 contains a frightening account of what might occur if you don't.)

- If you work for yourself, find out if the Data Protection Act requires you to register as a data collector. Unexpectedly few companies are exempt.

- Make plans for a daily off-site backup of your data, if necessary. It's just as awful to lose confidential information as it is to give it to the wrong people.

- Use caution when talking on your phone in a public setting; you never know who might be listening.

- When speaking with pals, refrain from casually bringing up your job or the people you interact with. When your professional and personal conversations take place in the same setting, sometimes even on the same phone, it's all too simple to accidentally bring up someone's name. If in doubt, avoid bringing up the subject or develop the practice of always following the Chatham House Rule to avoid saying something like, "So-and-so told me the other day.

THE CHATHAM HOUSE REGULATION

The Royal Institute of International Affairs is housed in Chatham House, and the Rule was established there almost a century ago to encourage open discourse on delicate subjects. The Chatham House Rule states, "Participants are free to use the information acquired at a meeting, or portion thereof, but neither the identity nor the affiliation of the speaker(s), nor that of any other participant, may be exposed."

In other words, you are allowed to share a specific piece of information but not the source of the information or the name of the organization to which the source belongs.

DELIVERING TOP-NOTCH CLIENT SERVICE

Although the individuals you work for might not directly compensate you for the work you do for them, we all have clients. People who live in your local authority region may be your customers if you work in the public sector, which is supported by government taxes. Alternatively, your clients could be your co-workers in the same or a different department who depend on your help while they provide a service.

According to reports, 70% of disgruntled consumers move their business elsewhere, not because they can get a better deal or locate a better product, but because they don't like the service they receive.

If you provide excellent customer service, you will be far more likely to retain your current clientele and avoid spending the time and resources necessary to acquire new ones.

Many books and millions of web pages have been written about the vast topic of customer service. I don't intend to cover every aspect of the topic in this article; instead, I'll only highlight a few that I've found to be particularly important for home-based workers and small business owners.

CONTINUOUSLY PROVIDE A GOOD EXPERIENCE

It's crucial that your clients can count on having a positive interaction with you every single time. Even if they like you, they will progressively cease returning if the quality is inconsistent.

SET YOURSELF APART IN THE MARKET

How many companies do you interact with on a personal or professional level that stand out from the competition? Not a lot, I bet. And how do you feel when you actually find one of these treasures? You make an effort to use it as frequently as possible and can't stop gushing about how fantastic it is. Being average may allow you to succeed to some extent, but where's the pleasure in that? When you can stand out from the crowd by making an extra effort, why blend in with everyone else?

In actuality, being unique doesn't require much effort. In some trades, simply showing up, to paraphrase Woody Allen, is enough to place you head and shoulders above the competitors. Emma's husband is a plumber, and occasionally after he has visited a client, she receives phone calls from that client saying, "People are quite astonished when my husband arrives up when we say he will." When I respond, "Yeah, that's correct, you were scheduled for today," they're just astounded and say, "Your spouse just came."

KEEP YOUR PROMISES BUT DELIVER MORE

When I ordered a book from Amazon, the significance of this became clear to me. They offer you a projected delivery date, so you mentally get yourself to wait till then. But the book arrived earlier than expected. One happy customer as a result. It's amazing how many firms get this incorrect because it's so simple to accomplish. Refrain from initially trying to appease your customer by providing an overly optimistic completion date if you are aware that fulfilling their request would take some time. Instead, make sure to estimate the time in advance so that when you deliver "early," the consumer is delighted and impressed by your efficiency.

DO WHAT YOU PROMISE TO DO

The customer's opinion of you is what matters, and they will judge you according to what you do, not what you say. Even though you profess a certain set of values and ideas, you could not act in a way that is consistent with them or communicate it to your customers. What matters is how your customer feels after dealing with you, not how you feel about your service or how you provide it. It is doubtful they will return if they have a bad impression.

MANAGE COMPLAINTS

Because we are only human, mistakes and oversights inevitably happen from time to time, so don't freak out if you receive a complaint. The manner in which you answer is more important than the existence of the complaint. A complaint is actually a chance to improve your relationship with that person or organization, just like you may have observed that conflict, as long as it is followed by resolution, brings friends and family members closer together.

Sometimes when I was running my cleaning service, a client would ring me and complain that a bin hadn't been emptied the night before. I always made a point of driving over to the office as soon as I could and emptying it personally, even though it wasn't a life-or-death emergency and could be fixed at the next clean.

demonstrate to my clients that their needs are essential to me and that I will respond to their requests quickly.

Not all complaints are as simply resolved, and occasionally the incident that prompted them has already happened and cannot be reversed. Then, inquire with the client, "What can I do to make it up to you? " or "How can I restore your faith in me?" Do whatever they suggest even though they could have an unexpected idea (within reason, of course).
Your response will make them so happy that they'll forget about their complaint.

STAY IN CONTACT

You are aware of how unsettling it is when you order something or request a service from a business or tradesperson and receive no response? After some time, you begin to distrust the terms of the agreement and wonder if they have forgotten or perhaps never wanted the business in the first place. If I have to do the chasing, I always feel little resentful. I am the client, so shouldn't they be vying for my business? Use these channels to stay in touch with your clients.

- Call them out of politeness to confirm appointments or simply to let them know you're keeping an eye on things even if there isn't any news yet.

- Update your client if the scheduled date changes. I'm not saying you shouldn't work hard to meet deadlines, but if you're having trouble finishing on time, give someone a quick call to see if they can give you a deadline extension.

- Regularly check your messages and respond to phone calls right away.

- Keep in mind the more traditional forms of communication; sometimes calling is quicker and easier than emailing, and snail mail still has its purpose.

- Ensure that people can reach you quickly. Provide all of your contact information, including your phone number, fax number, business address, email address, and website URL, on all of your correspondence, including emails.

- Never just say "Hello" while answering the phone; always say your name and possibly your company name. That sounds utterly unprofessional and makes a poor first impression on business calls.

- Don't give young children the responsibility of answering the phone. Others may find it to be a huge turnoff, yet some people may find it charming. Teach older kids how to answer the phone and accept messages just like you would. It might be time to create a separate business line if your kids constantly use the phone. Teach older kids to answer the phone the same way you do and to take messages. Installing a second business line can be necessary if your kids often use the phone.

- Record messages on your phone and mobile device so people know they have reached the appropriate number, and update them to suit your current situation. For example, "I'll call you back when I get home," I'll check my messages and get back to you as soon as I can, but I'll be in a conference till Thursday, the 20th.

- See Chapter 5 for additional advice on how to manage your phone usage and respond to emails quickly.

- Business contacts or clients are unlikely to appreciate you for forwarding chain emails or jokes. A large percentage of emails that call for support for political causes, warn of viruses, or ask for assistance in finding the missing are spoofs, which is hard to believe.

Having the appropriate appearance and Behaviour

When you are working from home, no one will see what you are wearing.

does it matter what you wear? But, in this section, we're focused on situations where people will see you, such as in your home office or while you're out in public. Clothes actually have a significant impact on mood and confidence, and their impact on productivity is covered in Chapter 5.

Many studies have demonstrated that our initial impressions of new people are exceedingly difficult to change. These perceptions are formed during the first few minutes of meeting someone. The appropriate impression must be given to your clients, colleagues, and the general public by your appearance and behaviour.

The appropriate image obviously begins with what you wear and how you present yourself, but it also encompasses much more.

THE RIGHT ATTIRE

Wearing attire appropriate for your profession is always a good idea, even when it seems apparent. It's not only a matter of appearance; wearing inappropriate attire will make people doubt your suitability for the position and will make them think less of you.

Ask someone who is always well-groomed for suggestions if you're unsure of what to dress or what suits you. If you're unsure whether to enlist the assistance of friends – and Several department stores provide a complimentary personal shopper who will handpick a selection for you to test from across the store, but the risk is that you wind up being their clone. There is typically no pressure to buy, but they should provide objective feedback as opposed to making you feel pressured. If you think you could use some moral support or a second opinion, your pal might be helpful.

Although hiring a professional colour consultant may seem pricey, I have yet to meet anyone who regretted the purchase. Your appearance and confidence are greatly improved by dressing in colours that flatter and inspire you, whether you're a man or a woman. Inquire as to whether the session will include address the type of clothing that best complements your body form, such as fitted or more flowing. By refusing to purchase anything that doesn't flatter you, you'll save a ton of money and wonder how you kept making the same mistakes in the past.

PROPER HYGIENE

Considering all the men's and women's grooming products available nowadays, it would seem unnecessary to bring up personal hygiene, but the reality is that I occasionally run into folks at work who have poop on their clothes, foul breath, or untidy hair. That kind of person is probably not reading this book because they are so ignorant, but perhaps if you know one, you'd like to add a bookmark to this website and forward it to them. But seriously, stressful situations like interviews and challenging meetings may literally make us perspire, as does summertime public transportation, so be ready and avoid being the focus of office rumours. I had to give an employee the "I'm afraid you smell" lecture many years ago while working as a personnel officer, and it was really awkward.

BAD ACTIONS

I once met a successful businessman who was well-liked by everyone he knew, but I know I wasn't the only one to notice this man's propensity to continuously itch his groin. We all have unconscious behaviours that come to the surface when we're anxious. Unless someone points them out to us or until we're caught on camera at work, we are completely ignorant of these patterns. Most people don't go quite as far as I did, but habitual hair pulling, nose picking, and jewellery playing can be grating and damage your professional image. Furthermore, if the last two are carried out by women, they could give a professional encounter a flirting touch that is quite undesired.

EQUIPMENT AND ACCESSORIES

Consider the minor details as well because whatever you wear or take around with you says as much about you as your clothing does. I've listed my top five fashion faux pas below.

- Pay attention to your shoes. Even though you may not be paying them any attention, others are. Maintain them clean, shiny, and in good condition. If you don't wear the same pair of shoes two days in a row, they will last longer.

- Wear only the barest minimum of jewellery, whether you're a man or a woman.
  Men who wear a bit too much jewellery could come out as Del-boyish. It
  suffices to wear a stylish watch, cufflinks, and a wedding band.

- Women don't improve their professional image with clattering bracelets that require regular restraining, fingers piled high with rings, and a collection of necklaces. Despite this, wearing a necklace or scarf is thought to boost women's self-confidence since it covers the throat, a particularly exposed area of the body. When I was a business adviser, I had a favourite set of big silver shield-shaped earrings that I wore every day if I anticipated a challenging day because they made me feel ready for fight.

- Ladies, don't even display your bra; don't show cleavage. Recently, exposing flesh has gotten considerably more accepted, but I'd still save it for your free time. Really, when you talk sales numbers, do you want your business partners to be looking down your shirt? The length of your skirt also conveys a lot of information about you; if it's too short, you risk looking edgy, while if it's too long, you look hippy-dippy. Maybe for safety's sake, so many professional women wear pants.

- Gentlemen, avoid wearing "jokey" socks or ties—those with cartoon figures and bright colours. While most people merely think they seem extremely sad, other people argue that they demonstrate what a wag you are.

- Your briefcase, laptop, mobile device, and handbag all contribute to your appearance, so choose them wisely and maintain their quality. I once purchased a nice leather briefcase while working in the cleaning profession, but I quickly stopped using it because I thought it suggested I was confined to an office, which was completely at odds with how I operated my business. I went back to a vibrant African basket instead, which contained all of my necessities, including extra cleaning products.

CARS

Whether you drive a business car or your personal vehicle, it's always a good idea to keep it clean both inside and out because you never know when you'll be requested to pick up the managing director or a significant client. I'm afraid anyone with pets or young kids are at a disadvantage here, and there's no escaping the reality that smokers' automobiles smell awful to non-smokers.

ETIQUETTE

The term "etiquette" may seem archaic, but it simply refers to the ability to put other people at ease in social or professional settings by showing consideration for them. Your reputation in the industry will improve if you can pull that off.

TIME KEEPING

Chapter 2 looks at potential explanations for why some people are able to consistently be on time while others are frequently late. If you're one of the unfortunate people who struggles to be punctual, you'll end up working very hard to make up for all the respect you've lost from irritated co-workers if you don't offer yourself enough reminders, such as setting the alarm on your mobile device.

Business Lunches

These tips may assist you to feel at ease, make a good impression, and even enjoy yourself when you go out for business meals with individuals you don't know very well.

- Turn off your phone as you enter the restaurant because it's simple to forget once the introductions and welcomes begin.

- The individual who proposed the gathering often foots the bill for the dinner. Take turns paying the tab if you two ever cross paths again. Ask when you get there if you're unsure of how the bill will be divided. Delaying it can make you anxious and result in one of those awkward "No, please, I insist" exchanges.

- If someone else is paying, choose an item on the menu that is in the middle of the price range rather than one of the most expensive options. Ordering messy cuisine (hold the spaghetti Bolognese) or challenging foods that you are unfamiliar with at this time is not recommended.

- Let your host to initiate conversation, and wait to bring up business until he does.

- As many business meals are conducted without alcohol, you should follow your host's example and refrain from drinking if you are the only one. Desserts fit into this as well. Drink in moderation if alcohol is present.

- If you are not pleased with your meal and don't know your host well, you can decide to overlook the error in favour of building a positive rapport. You should let your host know about your worry and allow them to discuss it with the waiter if there is a major issue or if you already know them well.

- Follow up the meal with a thank you email, call, or note, just like you would with any other networking activity, and carry out any commitments you made over the meal.

- If you are arranging the arrangements, ask your visitors how much time they have available and choose the location accordingly. Preferably, go someplace you are familiar with and know will be a positive experience. For business lunch patrons, some restaurants offer speedy service. You may wish to avoid congested areas and places with a lot of noise.

- Visit a location where you have already established a positive rapport with the workers before an important meeting. If you have a special request, like as a table in a private area where you can be unheard, talk to the management or head waiter in advance.

- If you receive good service, be sure to tip generously so that your guests will think highly of you.

Entertaining

Every Christmas, periodicals like newspapers and magazines publish the same how-to pieces. At the office party, act properly. Don't try to kiss the temp, photocopy your bottom, or get really wasted. By now, we are all familiar with the rules, but understanding them which we preserve). But what about social events hosted by colleagues or networking organizations when the rules don't seem to be as important? Is there still a need for a little propriety, or can you just relax and unwind? Once, I received an invitation to a party from a business acquaintance who also received several other business invitations. While trying to convince his guests to consume copious amounts of booze as well, he spent the evening getting very inebriated. Because of his boyish behaviour, I was unable to have positive feelings about him in his professional capacity. Keep drinking nights with close relatives and friends only; they are the ones most inclined to overlook inappropriate behaviour.

Express Gratitude

One of the most effective—and all too frequently forgotten—ways to leave a positive impression is by simply saying "thank you." We have a tendency to take for granted the things that go well in our haste to complete tasks and only become enthused about the difficulties and hiccups. I kept learning this in the cleaning company where we might clean an office for months without hearing a word, but I'd get a phone call from someone complaining if a tiny detail was missed once. No news is good news in this company, I used to tell my cleaners, but of course they lost motivation if they received no praise from our clients.

In contrast to the time and effort required to pick up the phone, send an email, or write a card, people value being acknowledged for the work they perform.
(Chapter 2 details the appropriate ways to express gratitude to different people.) And from a purely selfish standpoint, the best way to ensure that someone continues to provide the goods is to express your appreciation for them. I'm aware that every time someone has appreciated my work, it has strengthened my resolve to treat them with respect going forward.

WORKING WITH PEOPLE ELSEWHERE

Due to the strength and reach of the internet and modern communications, the world has become smaller, and it is now rather normal for even tiny enterprises to do business with people all over the world. It's important to understand that the practices and values we take for granted in our society may be very different in other countries since you may occasionally be obliged to meet them in person. Do your study before you travel to prevent offending someone and not even realizing it. In other regions of the world, far more importance may be placed on hierarchy, credentials, or family.

PLANNING

Know your stuff

The classic Boy Scout maxim, "Be prepared," also holds true for the homebody. Simply because you work from home doesn't mean you shouldn't be fully informed about your own business, its rivals, business partners, industry advancements, and potential future trends. You never know who you could run into and wish to impress at a networking event or even at the school gates.

Stock up

Along with being aware of pertinent facts, it's a good idea to keep extra supplies of your gear on hand so you can handle a sudden rush or a malfunction. Have a backup supply of paper and stock, and refer to Chapter 9 for disaster planning.

Keeping up with the times while working

Working from home has a risk that it won't advance your career or increase your prospects of promotion, either because business culture sees it as a sign of less dedication ('something women do after having kids') or because you are less visible to your superiors. For the benefit of your mental health and professional advancement, it's imperative that you stay up to date on office news and advancements when working from home.

- There is always someone in the office who is aware of what is happening. Determine who that person is, whether it be the receptionist or someone you don't work with directly, and stay in touch with them frequently.

Find out how they prefer to be acknowledged and let them know you value them in that way (see Chapter 2).

- Motivate your co-workers to stay in touch by making frequent phone and email calls to them.

- Attend all team meetings and training sessions if you are close to the office so that you may interact with other team members and show them that you are still an active team member.

- In a same vein, attend all social gatherings, evenings out, birthday parties, Christmas dinners, and business events.

- Be careful to maintain the required corporate image when you visit the office or go out to meet clients, regardless of what you decide to wear in the privacy of your workspace. There are several very strict clothing codes. If his sales people turned up in anything other than a simple, dark suit and white shirts, the senior manager of a blue-chip company he worked for was known for escorting them to Marks and Spencer's to purchase them. His best-selling book about small businesses demonstrates that there was a method to his craziness. No matter how well-presented, individuals are more inclined to buy from someone wearing these garments and colours than they are from someone wearing brown, according to Michael Gerber's The E Myth Revisited.

You must come up with strategies for effective communication with your manager, especially when it comes to sharing your accomplishments and high level of productivity.

- Learn about their interests so you can predict their dispositions and the most effective moment to approach them. A devoted football fan is likely to be miffed the day after his team suffers a crushing loss.

- Treat your management the same way you would a consumer, and try to anticipate their wants so you can respond to them before they even ask.

- Your responsibility is to make your manager appear good, so consider how you may do so most, with both their personal and professional goals. They will assist you more as long as you do.

- Tell them success stories so they can impress their employers. If you seem nice, your employers will too.

- Don't withhold unpleasant news, but consider potential solutions before to telling them.

- Spend time learning their preferred method of communication (see Chapter 2). Do they favour communication over email for information? Do they like to meet for lunch or coffee? How many specifics do they require?

Self-employed should have consistent branding

I had read that it takes seven "touches," or mentions or glimpses of your firm, before the general public learns something about you and what you do. These seven touches must all convey the same message in order for you to reach your target audience. You can communicate in a variety of methods, such as through the car you drive, advertisements placed in diverse locations like the local paper or on the back of a bus, your staff's uniform, website, business cards, correspondence, signs posted at the location you are working on, and so on.

No matter how tiny your company is, your branding or identity should carefully express what you do and how you conduct business. By making astute colour, typography, and logo choices, you may convey all of this and more. If you can afford it, you should consult a professional designer since they will know how people perceive colour and design, what is memorable, and what is most likely to motivate people to make a purchase. If money is very tight, a straightforward design won't need to be expensive.

After choosing an appropriate identity, the work is not done because anything bearing your logo needs to be neat and presentable. I said in Chapter 3 that my own cleaning company developed as a result of an effort to improve the stereotype of a window cleaner. As Emma and her husband own a plumbing company, they are well aware of the stereotype of a plumber as a guy in a flat cap and a beat-up automobile. We aim to provide a very different picture. To that purpose, they wash the van once a week, and Emma makes sure everything she sends out—including estimates, letters, and invoices—is well-written and properly spelled.

Nobody needs to know that you run a small business out of your home if you have a strong corporate image. Emma says it again: "Occasionally, people call and request that "someone" come out to them, as if we have a crew of plumbers. Oh, it's just my husband, I don't say. When I say, "My husband will come and see you," they assume I'm the boss.

Making sure that the tangible representations of your company have the appropriate image is not enough. Even more likely to harm or improve your reputation are the folks you hang out with.

THE IMPACT STAFF HAS ON YOUR PROFESSIONAL IMAGE

Chapter 3 addresses the paperwork and legal requirements associated with hiring employees.

But, the human element of hiring, educating, and overseeing personnel deserves significant attention on its own. There is no distinction between you, your company, and your employees in the eyes of the general public or your clients. Your employees represent your company to the general public, and they have the power to elevate your reputation with a well-placed comment or damage it with an inappropriate one.

Recruiting and keeping exceptional employees is by no means simple, and the lack of qualified part-time cleaners was the key factor in my decision to sell my company. Many small firms have grown to accommodate more employees only to contract back down when the workload got too much. By adhering to these recommendations, you'll get off to the finest start.

- Exercise judgment. Hiring a buddy of someone you know can sometimes be successful, but you frequently end up having to adjust your schedule to fit their preferences for hours and tasks. Identify what you need an employee to perform, how they should do it, when, where, and for how much money. Wherever you believe that person has the most chance of seeing it, post the job opening. It might appear in the local newspaper, at the Job Centre, in the window of the corner store, or in all three.

- Verify that respondents who respond meet all the requirements. Many people will apply in the hopes that you'll switch their shift to Thursday because you don't actually want them to work on Wednesdays. Invite the people on your shortlist who best fit your needs to a meeting. See Chapter 4 for alternatives if doing this at home doesn't appeal to you.

- If some candidates fail to show up for the interview, it is unlikely that they will do well. So, you shouldn't be too disappointed. To clear up any misunderstandings, restate the job description, the hours, and other pertinent information at the beginning of the interview. To catch any hints about their eligibility or desire for the job, pay close attention to what they say and how they say it during the conversation. When someone offers to quit their current job without giving their employer the full notice time, don't take them up on it; if they're prepared to do it to their current employer, they'll do it to you as well.

- After viewing each candidate, choose the one who, in your opinion, offers the best combination of experience, personality, desire for the position, readiness to learn, and any other key considerations. Making the "correct" decision is challenging, if not impossible; instead, aim for the decision that is best given your knowledge and intuition.

- Choose a start date for your top candidate and extend the offer. You might want to hold off on telling the other applicants they didn't get the job until they had already begun. If that is not possible, you might wish to explain that this particular position has been filled and that you will be in touch when a new one opens up.

- Get two references, ideally from current and former employers, or at the least, from someone you can trust to give an unbiased assessment. I wouldn't take the chance of hiring a candidate if they couldn't give me with two referees.

- On the first and subsequent days, provide them precise and concise instructions until you are satisfied that they understand their responsibilities. Instructions on how to interact with clients, the required level of language and appearance, the standard of driving and cars, and other topics should all be covered during training.

- I'll start by wishing you luck. Managing people is a challenging task. I'd like to think that if you treat your employees well, they would treat you and the job well, but I know that's not always the case. That also does not justify mistreating them. Each person needs to develop their unique style, which can only be achieved through practice.

SUPPLIERS' IMPACT ON YOUR PROFESSIONAL IMAGE

Price is not the only factor to take into account if you want to build and maintain a solid professional reputation, but it is crucial for all businesses to get the best deal possible on the items and services they purchase. It is inevitable that the local business community finds out who is doing business with whom, and it will reflect poorly on you if you surround yourself with people whose integrity is questionable. While selecting and conducting business with suppliers, keep these things in mind.

- Consider aspects other than just the lowest price. Is the company reputable and well-established? In the long term, that might be far more important to you.
- If your financial flow permits, pay them on promptly and in advance of the due date. We always take note of and value prompt payment.
- Express gratitude for a job well done and inform them of any issues, not just to complain but also to give them a chance to fix the situation.

- Pass their name along to others if you're pleased. The best (and most affordable) approach to gain new clients is through a word-of-mouth recommendation, and recipients will value it.
- They might refer you to others, so be sure to thank them if they do.

EFFECTIVENESS OF CLIENTS ON YOUR PROFESSIONAL IMAGE

All independent contractors and small businesses require customers, but it might be tempting to take any opportunity that presents itself, especially in the beginning. My personal experience,

speaking with other home schoolers informs me that more is not always better. Working for yourself seems to go more smoothly if you trust your instincts and only work with people you feel comfortable around in addition to avoiding sketchy personalities as stated in the section above on suppliers.

PART 3

SECRETS OF SUCCESS

7

WON'T I FEEL ISOLATED?

Brendan Barber, the general secretary of the TUC, claimed in 2007 that the UK has the longest workweeks in all of Europe, therefore it is not unexpected that the people we meet there play a significant role in our lives as co-workers, friends, and potential spouses. If you've always collaborated with others, you may be concerned about how you'll function if you work remotely.

The following are some of the topics covered in this chapter:

1.   How your ability to cope with the loneliness of working alone will determine
        how much you love working from home.

2.   You can stay linked by phone, email, and in-person meetings with passing
        acquaintances, friends, and co-workers, also enjoyable company are pets.

3.   Networking gets you outside of the house, provides assistance, and may lead
        to new business opportunities. Choose your group wisely and keep in mind
        that everyone was apprehensive when they first started networking.

4.   Internet networking gives you the opportunity to meet people locally as well

as globally, expanding your network of contacts.

Managing Isolation

Isolation is one of the major problems of working from home, and how you handle it will determine whether you can do so happily or not, according to the homeworkers I spoke with. Nobody else is nearby to converse with, debate the news with, or offer assistance when you're stuck.

How content you are working alone will rely on your personality, primarily on whether you are an extrovert or an introvert, as we discovered in Chapter 2. (If you haven't already, you might want to finish answering the questions in Chapter 2 before continuing.) But there will always be occasions when you want to interact with others, no matter how much you prefer being by yourself. Humans have a fundamental urge to feel connected to other people.

In the 1950s, American psychologist Abraham Maslow wrote his renowned Hierarchy of Needs, which has since evolved into a cornerstone of training and personal development. Maslow ranks the fulfilment of what he refers to as "belongingness and love needs" (which include work group, family, and other relationships) as the second most essential need after the "safety" need for security and stability and the "physical" need for oxygen, food, and water. In other words, your most urgent need is for friendship once you are warm, nourished, and hydrated, and pretty certain there aren't any nasty shocks threatening your survival.
The good news is that you don't actually have to work from home when you work from home because you may schedule

your job so that you can leave the house whenever you choose.

It is totally up to you as a home worker to arrange regular communication with those who can give you the drive and inspiration to stay motivated. This is the second most significant item after finishing your task in my opinion. When you are under pressure, it can be easy to put off meeting new people if you are content with your own company. Yet, without some outside support, you may quickly lose your momentum.

Keeping In Touch

"Remain in touch!" How often do we use this phrase? How frequently do we then fail to proceed with it? You will be more successful working from home if you maintain regular contact with a group of useful contacts. Some of these contacts may be able to introduce you to others, some may have skills that are complementary to your own, some may have good ideas, and others may be objective when you can't see the forest for the trees and will assist you in making decisions. There are several advantages to maintaining the contact because people like this can provide you a powerful and broad network. By offering you practical, emotional, and intellectual support when working alone, developing and maintaining a strong network will help you keep your sanity and perspective.

Be careful not to only call people when you need something from them (see Chapter 2, Thinking and Feeling); instead, ring to say hello and inquire about their lives.
Don't wait until there is a crisis because by then it will be too late and your network will quickly dwindle if you only

ever contact people to ask for favours. If time tends to fly by and you forget to do it, instead make a note in your diary.

Keep Chapter 2 in mind and consider how your various contacts might prefer to communicate. To discuss a shared professional interest, would they rather speak with you over the phone, meet for a cup of coffee, or schedule a formal meeting?
You can get the most out of them and keep life exciting for yourself by experimenting with different forms of communication. This chapter's remaining sections examine several methods for meeting potential network members. Depending on your profession and personality, you may undoubtedly run into a lot of additional situations.

GOING OUTSIDE MORE

Working in an office, you may have yearned to escape the individuals crammed into the train, shoving you in the street, or disturbing you at your work. That may have appeared like the ideal option to work in peace and quiet at home. Although working from home might increase productivity, as we saw in Chapter 5, you will grow to value human interaction in a way that you didn't when you commuted every day. My friend claims that she can tell she has been working alone for too long when a nice interruption, like a delivery, prompts her to start chatting with such vigour that the delivery person begins to hesitantly approach the gate!

When working from home, having good neighbours to spend the time with is quite helpful, and there are many other methods to add some light relief to your day. Here are a few more ideas that I've found to be effective.

NEARBY FACES

When you work in an office, you frequently run into the receptionist, cleaner, security guard, and woman who comes in to water the plants. They probably serve only as the backdrop to other activities. You will have a different set of familiar faces while you work from home, which you may come to cherish for the distraction they offer. You don't need to attend gatherings and events to get new energy and enthusiasm. Just conversing with the folks, you meet during the day has the potential to do this. The other parents at the school gates, the man working at the newsstand, your hairdresser, or the postman could all be the source.

FRIENDS AND FAMILY

Unless you were able to make personal calls while at work, your desk may have been the only reminder of your loved ones. Of course, when you are working, the individuals who know you best can offer sympathy and support. You may need to be disciplined and only contact them after hours if you want to avoid accidentally sending the message that you are always available. In the first few months, this may be vital as you work from home. In Chapter 8, we discuss how to set limits between work and family time as well as how to handle working with other family members.

PETS

When you spend your days at home, having a pet is a great idea. Dogs and cats are wonderful (and uncritical) companions and will enjoy having you around more. The

Blue Cross animal welfare charity conducted a survey of pet owners in 1999 and found that 89% of respondents said their animals helped them unwind, 96% said they helped them deal with loneliness, and 96% said they gave them friendship. Also, they can encourage you to go out of the house frequently and create and maintain an effective work schedule (see Chapter 5). Nonetheless, getting a new pet at the same time as you start working from home is not a good choice. Each of these adjustments are significant and demand a lot of dedication.

IF YOU ARE EMPLOYED

Consider the co-workers you used to interact with on a daily basis and make an attempt to be as visible as you can. Go to all the regular work events, such as the Christmas parties, leaving dos, training sessions, and meetings. You already have a ready-made network of co-workers, managers, and team members. When you are not physically present in the office every day, as discussed in Chapter 6, it maintains you in everyone's thoughts and boosts your personal morale. Staying in touch with previous co-workers and superiors when they transition to new positions helps widen your network even more.

IF YOU ARE SELF-EMPLOYED

Consider all the people you interact with on a daily basis at work. You might have to put in a little more effort creating your network than someone who has a job.
The persons on the list will include your customers, suppliers, workers, people who provide a comparable service, and so forth. Many of the self-employed folks you know work from home. Why not start a club that gathers on

a regular basis for lunch or coffee to discuss problems and news? You can choose to go to a convenient cafe or meet at each other's homes.

WORK SUPPORT

Along with the chance to socialize with co-workers during breaks and after-hours activities, working in an office environment offers support services of every sort that you never even consider. These services include an unending supply of stationery, raw materials, and technical assistance. It's possible that you'll have to plan everything on your own at home, so getting along with the guy who shows up when your computer breaks down may become more crucial. Being able to conduct regular business with individuals who are in the same situation is a pleasure of working independently from home.

A PHONE AND THE INTERNET

Of course, you don't have to physically meet people to develop a supporting network; you can do it from home using your phone, email, and online forums. However, I would highly advise you to make a point of scheduling regular get-togethers outside the home.

If you develop a routine for using your phone when working from home, depending on whether you make a lot of brief calls, call people abroad, or talk for an hour or more at a time, check to make sure you are on the best and lowest rate. You should be able to limit the amount of time you spend on your phone to when you have to leave the house while waiting for a call.

Gratis online calendars and address books like Plaxo alert users to forthcoming birthdays, update member contact information, and enable the sending of electronic greeting cards. Later in this chapter, we'll take a closer look at internet networking.

WHY ARE PEOPLE NETWORKING?

Doing regular exercise is one strategy to stay active and may also help with income generation.

Joining a networking group will help you get more business. I've noticed that hardly anyone will admit to like networking; instead, they usually pull their faces and say something like, "Yuck, networking, I detest it, but I suppose you have to do it."
Perhaps because so many people only link it with selling, this is the case. They attend a couple of professionally organized networking events, but are dismayed when no new sales result. They eventually give up and claim that "networking doesn't work" to you. I advise you to view networking as nothing more than a pleasurable diversion from work and a chance to meet some new people.

I don't think networking is about selling, and you'll do best if you don't have any expectations along those lines. I've frequently been greeted enthusiastically at networking gatherings by a recent business acquaintance who seemed happy to see me before subjecting me to a sales pitch. I feel terrible about this and am completely turned off by the person and their company.

See networking as being all about becoming well-known and loved. While this requires patience and persistence, the results are astounding. You might believe that you simply aren't the correct type of person to network. That's what I envisioned.

SELECTING YOUR NETWORKING GROUP

Around the nation, networking clubs have exploded over the past few years. There are now groups for all professions and industries, as well as for women, young entrepreneurs, the self-employed, and individuals living in rural areas, to name a few.

You have the option of joining as a self-employed individual or as an employee who works on behalf of your business. Contact your industry association, the neighbourhood Chamber of Commerce, your nearby Business Link office, or chat with your business bank manager to learn more about organizations in your area. The Resources section at the conclusion of the chapter contains additional information.

At breakfast, lunch, and after work, you can network. Some organizations only ask a little price to cover the cost of renting the space and providing refreshments, while others require a hefty yearly subscription. Take advantage of this opportunity to ask some direct questions of a variety of members before you commit because the later are more geared toward generating business and will only provide a little period where you can trial before you buy.

For instance, BNI (Business Networking International) requires its members to present business recommendations to each gathering. You may lack the depth of relationships to do this if you operate as a one-man operation, such as a business consultant with a small number of niche clientele. Some networks have highly rigorous attendance policies, and absent members are required to locate a replacement. The best way to test out the group is to fill in for an absent member.

Above all, resist being overly swayed by advertising that makes exaggerated promises about how much more business the network will bring in. Though the numbers given may be accurate, keep in mind that they are averages, and in my experience, some businesses perform remarkably well, sometimes to the extent that they are forced to leave the network due to a lack of work, while others perform abjectly and see little to no return on their investment. After attending your first event, and especially before committing, it can be helpful to ask yourself and other network members a few important questions.

Questions to pose to network participants

- How much business have you generated as a result of joining this network?
- What aspects of the group do you find appealing and objectionable?
- What types of companies gain the most from this network?
- Are there any other fees on top of the subscription?
- What happens if I have a complaint or a dispute against one of the members?
- What are the attendance regulations?
- What duties exactly do I take on if I join this group?

Before joining a networking organization, consider these questions.

- Were the current members friendly and welcoming to me?
- What do I think of the members' professionalism? Do they seem to be merely out to make a quick cash or would I be pleased to promote them to my relatives and friends? Do I want to be linked with these people?
- Was the meeting run efficiently, or was there some time lost?
- Are the references that members have provided appear sincere or are they fumbling to fill out the numbers?
- Does someone in the group naturally have a commercial connection with me? Web designer and computer hardware expert, mortgage adviser and will-planning service, graphic designer and printer, and others are examples of complementary businesses that can refer business to one another. You might not get many recommendations if you are a "one-off" in the group.

STARTING TO NETWORK

Even after you've attended a few networking events, you might still feel a little anxious. Attending your first few networking events can be nerve-wracking. In a flash of enthusiasm, I've noticed that I often commit to going to an event, but as the day draws near, I start to second-guess myself and start looking for excuses not attending. I've discovered that showing up as scheduled, stubbornly ignoring any doubts, and making an effort to not think about it are the best courses of action. Even when I worried about wasting time, I have never once regretted my choice. These are my tried-and-true advice for fast putting oneself at ease.

- Go with someone you know, preferably a seasoned networker who can introduce you to others, until you get acclimated to networking.
- Alternately, make plans to meet a colleague there so that you will at least know one person.
- Be very disciplined and try not to give in to the urge to talk to the people you know constantly during the event; after all, you are there to make new contacts.
- If you're coming alone, ask the receptionist to put you in touch with someone you want to meet or someone from a certain field you want to connect with as soon as you walk in.
- Keep in mind that everyone else at the event is probably just as scared as you are, or will recall that they once were. They want to talk to someone just as badly as you do.
- No matter how powerful they may be, never feel like you can't approach them since they are there to meet people too, and you might be just who they are searching for.
- When there is so much going on around you, it might be challenging to concentrate on your current companion, especially if you know you must leave shortly. Try to avoid acting like a "meerkat" by avoiding peering over your partner's shoulder and making them feel inferior.
- Being left alone at a networking event when everyone else is chatting in groups of two or three is challenging. Join a group right immediately without thinking twice. A trio is preferable because one of

them is likely feeling less involved than the others and will be happy to see you.

- There are times when a conversation comes to a natural conclusion and you are stuck for a courteous way to continue. Say something like, "It's been nice meeting you and I hope we'll run into each other again, but I mustn't monopolize you," to avoid spending the entire event with the same individual. Inquire if they can connect you with someone else.

- There are times when a conversation comes to a natural conclusion and you are stuck for a courteous way to continue. Say something like, "It's been nice meeting you and I hope we'll run into each other again, but I mustn't monopolize you," to avoid spending the entire event with the same individual. Inquire if they can connect you with someone else.

AFTER NETWORKING, TAKING ACTION

In all likelihood, you will have liked your time at the group, but don't just forget about it after you leave home, especially if you made a promise to email someone information during a conversation. Following up can be time-consuming, but it's worth it in the end:

- Express your pleasure at meeting each person you spoke with in an email the following day. Since I don't think networking is about selling, I find it annoying when people attach information about their business to this email. Consider whether this is appropriate and then make a decision.

- List the date and the occasion on the back of each card you collected to keep a record of what you discussed. Then, file the cards. Before the subsequent event, you can have a short glance at them. Being remembered makes people happy.

- Send someone whatever information you can think of, such as a webpage or an article, that they would find helpful. You can create a strong network if you are prepared to lend a hand to others without expecting anything in return.

- Schedule additional contact in accordance with the circumstance and the temperament of your interaction. If you're unsure whether a card, phone call, or meeting would be most appropriate, have a look at Chapter 2, page 28.

WEB-BASED NETWORKING

By joining a neighbourhood networking organization, you can meet people in your neighbourhood. Joining an online network will put you in touch with people you would never otherwise have the opportunity to meet from all over the world. You might want to check out the business networks Ryze, Xing, Ecademy, and LinkedIn. Now, businesspeople use popular social networking sites like Facebook and Myspace. I have encountered both online networking believers and people who don't fully comprehend the concept. Your response may vary depending on how much you take pleasure in internet activities. Online networking certainly isn't for you if you're the type of person who can't wait to put your computer down after work, even if many online groups also host in-person activities. Before committing, keep the following things in mind.

- Check out established, sizable organizations as a guest first, such as Ecademy and LinkedIn. You can join special interest clubs on large networks, or you can search for a niche network that is relevant to your field or interests.

- The adage "more you put in, the more you are likely to get out" is true for both offline and online networking. It will therefore probably take some time, at least initially. You will be needed to submit your contact information as well as a profile of your life and work.

- Despite how tempting it is to quickly put something up and start networking, take the time to write a clear and intriguing profile before proofreading it for errors in spelling and punctuation. They will judge you properly because this is how you are introduced to the networker community. Keep updating your profile as your work progresses and as new information becomes available.

- Be ready for an onslaught of welcome emails from zealous networkers who get in touch with each new member in an effort to widen their own network. If someone isn't particularly interesting to you and requires a personalized answer, you can save time by responding with a typical email.

- The more contacts you have, the better, is how online networks work. According to Thomas Power, the founder and chairman of Ecademy, you may make £100,000 a year if you have 1000 people in your network. Whatever the case, it's important to strike a balance between time spent networking and time spent working and managing your local network.
- Avoid sending hasty emails because it's easier to be harsh or critical online than in person and it's frequently difficult to tell the tone of an email you receive. It is preferable to wait and read your manuscript again before sending. Additionally keep in mind that not just the intended recipients but also many others may view any online communication. Your customers, managers, and other influential figures in your field may be included in it.

- Some smaller networks are only there to provide support to their users by exchanging information. Clare was able to hire three highly qualified staff when she moved her company from the city to the country (see Chapter 1) simply by sending an email on her local network for women in business, saving a large amount on advertising expenses.

8

HOW DO I KEEP HOME AND WORK SEPARATED?

Individuals frequently prefer to work from home in an effort to achieve a better work/life balance, but when work and family obligations coexist in the same space, it can be challenging to set clear boundaries. Your perception of "home" will change once your employment is done from home. It is no longer a haven from the chaos of life, a place where you can lock the door, unwind, and just be yourself, but rather a place where you must deal with all facets of work, even the tedious and irksome.

This chapter discusses:

1.   How to take care of your own emotional, mental, and physical health
2.   How to maintain your connections with friends and family.
        It is ideal to study these sections in conjunction with Chapter 5, which discusses setting up a schedule and working productively from home (because they compliment one another).
3.   Making adjustments to your connection with your partner, regardless of
        whether they commute or do their work from home.
4.   Strategies for setting and maintaining limits with kids and teenagers.
5.   Your customers are paying for the experience when they enter your home.

While working from home, you should take care of yourself

TAKING CARE OF YOUR MENTAL AND EMOTIONAL WELL-BEING

You create a helpful emotional and mental distance between your home and your workplace when you leave for work. Whether you're a secretary, designer, or builder, you do this by dressing for the job at hand, adopting your work persona, and spending the day "in character." You have some emotional shelter from your job persona, which also makes it easier for you to brush off some of the minor or upsetting things that happen to you there. When you go home, you take off your clothing, drop your guard, and resume being the "genuine" you with your loved ones. You also remove your protective shell and work persona.

When you work from home, you are less protected since you don't have the office environment to fall back on. You might have been hanging out the laundry when that unpleasant client called to yell at you. Your home and your troubles may begin to seem contaminated by your co-workers' emotions and issues as they begin to bother you about issues you may have easily overlooked in the office.

On the other hand, if there are issues at home, going to work can be a relief. Taking a day trip can help you put things in perspective and distract you from your problems. On the other side, staying put may keep you in close proximity to the person(s) you would prefer to see less of while also continually reminding you of what's wrong. The fact that you work in a familiar atmosphere where a variety of events could cause a mood swing or that nobody has tidied up their breakfast dishes or that you received a call from your mother at an inappropriate moment can make you feel downright pessimistic when you should be feeling cheery

YOUR MOOD CHANGE

It's critical to be as optimistic and self-assured as you can to produce the finest professional results, thus it's crucial that you are conscious of your emotional and mental states and have some degree of control over them. The goal is to become conscious of your emotions and realize that you can stop blaming others for your problems and shift your mindset to one that is more productive, whether you need to make a phone call or prepare a report. It may first appear impossible to break free from years of ingrained behaviour because we aren't taught to do this as children, but it simply takes practice.

You may come to the realization that you need to change your negative and depressed feelings to ones that are upbeat and confident. Consider the most recent instance when you felt really confident, and carefully recall the experience. Make the event as real as you can by keeping in mind who was there, what you were wearing, where you were, what you and they were saying, and what you were saying to yourself. Use all of your senses, including the texture of the chair you are sitting in, the taste of the meal you are eating, and any aroma you may be able to detect.

Just thinking about it will produce the same sentiments of assurance because the mind is unable to distinguish between fact and imagination. Don't image yourself in the situation as you imagine it; instead, see it through your own eyes as if you were actually there and taking in everything exactly as it was. With practice, you'll begin to feel confident once more, and eventually, you'll only need to recall that one experience to regain your confidence.

You might not be able to recall a moment when you felt that way if you're truly sad, so try to picture how it might feel. Alternatively, you might imagine the actions and feelings of someone who exudes confidence in your own abilities.

UNDERSTANDING HOW TO RESPOND WHEN SOMEONE IRRITATES YOU

Making conclusions about others based on their behaviour is common.
Perhaps you had the impression that someone had just given you an extremely rude phone call. Your initial thought will usually be one of two things: either they are incredibly rude, in which case you don't like them very much, or they don't like you for whatever reason. In either case, the interaction might have left you feeling bad, yet either outcome could be wholly off the mark.

The Seven Habits of Highly Effective People, Stephen Covey's best-selling book, contains a tale about this. He was riding the train in New York when a dad and his two kids boarded. While his kids wreaked havoc outside the carriage, the dad sat down next to him and closed his eyes. When Covey could take no more, he urged the man to keep them under control. The man opened his eyes and said, "I know I should do something, but we just came from the hospital where my wife passed away, and I don't know what to do." Covey's displeasure, as you might expect, quickly subsided.

So instead of assuming the worst when people don't treat you how you'd like, why not? Assume they've just received some bad news or are having a terrible day and give them the benefit of the doubt.

A SENSE OF GUILT

Susy moved her office out of central London and into a cottage in the countryside.
a conservatory Sounds great, but she claims that if she is working, the garden needs to be organized and the opposite is true.

One of the worst things about working from home is that when you finish a task at work, you step away from your desk and are immediately reminded that the dishes need to be done, the grass needs to be cut, or the pantry needs to be stocked with food. Yet, if you take too long to resolve it, you begin to consider the tasks you're ignoring in your office.

Women certainly appear to experience this constant guilt more strongly than males, especially when children are involved, but I say this with hesitation since I don't want to enter into the classic "multitasking" debate. Women multitask a lot, even if it's just in their brains, while males appear to be able to focus solely on one thing at a time.

The notion that working from home is such a luxury that they must make a sacrifice or otherwise justify its advantages to someone—perhaps themselves, their partners, or their employers—is another strange form of guilt that plagues those who used to commute to work. All the time they had been spending traveling is suddenly available to them, and they believe it needs to be used wisely. This, in my opinion, is one of the factors contributing to homemakers' higher productivity.

The tendency to feel guilty seems to be just one of the drawbacks of working from home, but it does get easier with time.

HOW TO GET HELP

No matter how happy you are to be alone, there will be times when you need the companionship and stimulation of being around others. If you haven't already, look at Chapter 7 for suggestions on how to get out and meet people.

THE ABILITY TO SWITCH OFF WHEN NEEDED

It can be difficult to put your work on hold when you need to and to turn your mind away from it during downtime if your workspace is readily available to you at home. Even when you're tempted to keep working, it's easier if you schedule your break in advance and stick to it. Homeworkers typically pick up this skill through trial and error, often by pushing themselves too far before realizing their actions were counterproductive. In order to prevent incoming calls from disturbing your leisure, it is a good idea to turn off the computer and, if possible, reduce the level of the answer phone. Yet, thanks to the technology we have at our disposal, like mobile phones, BlackBerrys, and wireless networks, you can go practically anywhere and still get calls or emails. If you run a firm where clients could call at any time to seek for your assistance with an emergency, it might be quite difficult to entirely switch off.

Sometimes it's impossible to switch off since work and life are so linked. Perhaps you might discover that once you start working from home, the lines between work and leisure time start to melt in a positive way and that your attitudes about "work time" and "relaxation time" are different.

TAKING CARE OF YOUR PERSONAL HEALTH

Many individuals worry that being home all day with continual access to food and drink will cause them to become overweight and slothful since working from home means losing the external discipline that forces you to get up, dress for work, leave the house on time, and eat at set break times. Working from home requires some discipline, but taking care of your physical well-being need not be any more difficult than avoiding the cakes and chips at the office.

Diet

It can be a concern if you're so close to the kitchen and refrigerator. It's all too easy to make coffee breaks and snacks a regular part of your working day, turning to them when you're feeling uninspired or as a reward for finishing a challenging task. To work from home without gaining weight, use these tips:

- Avoid food shopping when you're hungry; it's a common advice, but it truly does help. It's difficult to resist the current BOGOFs and your favourite goodies when your stomach is growling.

- Refusing to eat all those treats once you get home is much easier than it is to leave them on the grocery store rack. If necessary, avoid that area of the shop entirely because you are aware of your limitations.

- If you're on the verge of giving in, visualize bumping into the last person you'd want to run into with all those pleasures in your basket as soon as you reach the checkout. Maybe a member of your workout class, your personal trainer, or your neighbour, who is trim and well-groomed.

- As usual, self-awareness is the key, so pay attention to the times of day you feel the most peckish and the times you are most likely to be tempted by fatty or sugary snacks. Afterward, you can adjust your eating habits accordingly. Even if you don't want much for breakfast, you can be ravenous by noon. Eating your big meal then and a little snack later will help you maintain your weight loss.

- Don't completely eliminate out your favourite calorie-dense foods; doing so could make you feel deprived and cause you to binge. Consume in moderation, for example, by ordering a slice of cake when you go out for coffee rather than a full cake. When you are dining with other people, it is simpler to manage your intake because no one wants to appear to be a gluttonous.

- If you do have enticing foods at home and you are unsure of your ability to resist them, there is no guilt in asking your partner to hide and ration them.

Exercise

- If your job requires a lot of sitting down, get up and move about frequently. Otherwise, you risk becoming slumped over time, which will lower your mood. The body and mind will benefit from being outside in the fresh air. Sue attends three gym courses a week, saying, "I may not speak to anyone while I'm there, but I really look forward to stretching and pushing myself." Sue claims she is "chomping at the bit" to leave the house after working hours. I'm healthier than I've ever been.

- You are more likely to continue with regular exercise if you incorporate an exercise class, session, or trip to the gym or pool into your daily schedule. You have access to sports facilities during quiet times of the day and can attend a variety of daytime classes, unlike your office-bound co-workers.

- By strolling around the block or taking the dog for a walk, you can use activity to start your day and/or signal when you are turning off.

- Rebounders (small trampolines) are wonderful for exercising without even needing to put on shoes and leave the house, making them perfect for winter. Just transition from annoyance to cheeriness is another fast and efficient technique to lift your mood. Bounce to energetic music to maintain momentum and instantly improve your mood.

Re-energisers

Sometimes you just need a little boost of energy to get you through to the deadline or mailing of the letter. You are not required to leave your desk or even rely on caffeine.

- When you're feeling down, press the thumb of your other hand against the centre of your palm to jolt yourself back to life. By pressing below the ball of your foot, you can achieve the same result if you're feeling flexible.

- Eyes grow tired from staring at a computer for extended periods of time, so make it a practice to blink frequently. To give your eyes a break, gaze out the window into the distance before gazing at something close-up, like your hand.

- Take a deep breath! Breathe three times deeply— three times into your lungs, not just your chest. Alternately, try the purifying breath used in yoga to flush out toxins and oxygenate the brain: inhale for 4 counts, hold the breath for 2, exhale for 6 counts, hold the breath for 2 counts, and repeat.

- Pulling up the top of your ears while holding the tops in place will activate the acupuncture points on your ears. Up until the lobes, work all the way around the edge. Then, let go after pulling them down firmly.

- To relieve jaw tension, yawn widely, say "Aaah," and gently massage the jaw's hinge, which is located just above the ear.

Exercise Programs

In addition to being a terrific way to unwind at the end of the week or reward yourself for completing a challenging job, massage, reflexology, shiatsu, and many other therapies are both physically and mentally healthy for homeworkers.
To continue honing their craft, therapists frequently trade sessions with one another. As a result, they may be amenable to the concept of trading their knowledge for yours, such as a massage or series of massages for some bookkeeping tasks.

Illness

It's simple to call in sick when you're working away from home and feeling a little off. Nobody is aware of your condition, and you will yet be compensated. In contrast to what you might expect, homeworkers are less likely to want to stay in bed. As was indicated in the part above on feeling guilty, people who work from home seem to feel like they have something to prove. If you're self-employed, the desire to continue working is much greater because you could not be paid while off sick.

It is certainly feasible to work while taking naps and medication; in fact, I did so while experiencing a kidney illness, though I now believe I must have been insane at the time. However, taking a few days off would give your mind and body the chance to heal more rapidly. The best test to use is whether you would miss work if you were working outside the home while you were ill. and proceed as such.

TAKING CARE OF FAMILY AND FRIENDS

Despite the fact that you like them and enjoy spending time with them, you may need to establish some ground rules to make sure they understand that you are working even when you are at home. Use the following ideas to gently persuade them they shouldn't frequently show up or call during business hours:

- If your home and business lines are distinct, it is probably simpler to leave your home line on voicemail during the day and just pick up after work.

- If you just have one phone line, make sure you always greet callers with a professional business greeting during the day. Hopefully, this will serve as an immediate reminder to family and friends that you are on duty and should not be bothered by social affairs. Tell them you have a deadline to meet or that you're anticipating a crucial call and that you'll call them back after the day's work is done if they appear insistent on conversing.

- The phrases "I'd better let you go" or "I mustn't keep you" are effective when you need to stop a call quickly and politely without offending anyone. They are not the one who might be a bother.

- A greeting along the lines of "How nice to see you and such a shame I can't invite you in" should be used if someone unexpectedly knocks on your door.

I'm already behind schedule and have a deadline to meet. Will you be available

on phone to make correct plans later? I only do it if I am actually on a call, in case someone decides to call me right then and there! Some individuals advise opening the door with a cell or cordless phone glued to your ear.

- If you ever plan a get-together during regular business hours with a friend or relative, be sure to let them know that you are taking a vacation or taking the day off, and let them know when the regular plans will continue.

(If you haven't read Chapter 5 yet on creating a schedule and being productive at home, it could be helpful to do so now as much of the information there is related to this.)

MAINTAINING YOUR PRIMARY RELATIONSHIP

You're aware of the statistics claiming to estimate the stress levels of life events like divorce, bereavement, and moving? You should consider starting to work from home with your partner as a significant life transition and make plans appropriately. As far as I know, nobody has yet attempted to calculate the level of stress suffered by starting to work from home. It's crucial to understand that you might not immediately achieve equilibrium because working from home may affect your separate responsibilities in ways you didn't anticipate.

When you work from home, things in your relationship tend to get blown out of proportion because tiny annoyances seem more significant.
Communication is essential for maintaining personal ties while working from home, just as it is for using computers and phones for communication.
Follow these recommendations to make the switch to homeworking as easy as possible.

- Even though you may have been waiting for this day for a very long time, remember that it will likely take some time for everyone to adjust.

- Consider all the alterations to your home and your management style that working from home may entail. Decide who will be responsible for each task as you go through your typical workday, including getting breakfast, dropping off the kids at school, doing the laundry, ironing, planning meals, shopping, cooking, cleaning, and so on.

- Despite having agreed upon responsibility for each task, you may need to be flexible in practice if circumstances or the demands of the job call for periodic changes in responsibilities.

- Try not to "keep score" by saying things like, "I've been doing the cooking all week and you're just sitting there in front of the TV." Focusing on how much you're doing compared to how little your partner does makes you resentful and judgmental, and every time I give in to it, I later realize I've missed out on a kind, unselfish deed and have further embroiled myself in trouble. Not worth the risk.

- But do vent your resentments as soon as they surface. Even if you believe that speaking up would make you appear petty or juvenile, don't wait until you can no longer contain your anger and it erupts in a fit of rage. Try saying, "I know this isn't logical/rational/grown-up, but I feel resentful/envious/cross about you going on that business trip/leaving early so I have to prepare the kids/be here all the time on my own." Simply getting these poisonous little thoughts out in the open can make everything feel so much better, but letting them fester only makes the issue worse.

- Learn how and what makes your partner angry when you ask them to do anything. I often obliquely request things because I'm afraid of coming off as demanding. For example, "I'm becoming hungry now, are you?" actually means, "Please will you get lunch ready because I'm concentrating on this and I need food very soon or I'll get extremely grumpy." That irritates my partner, who, if he's feeling contrary, will just acknowledge that he is growing a little peckish and continue working because, after all, I never asked him to do anything. Eliminating these minor irritations will save a lot of time and many wasted tempers.

PROVIDING AND OBTAINING FEEDBACK

Honest communication is necessary to discuss all of these issues, but even with our closest friends and family members, it can be challenging. Learning how to give and receive feedback is one method to promote effective communication and keep it going. Even though you may occasionally wish to do so, by feedback I don't only mean criticism of your partner's performance or behaviour. In order to make life as organized and pleasurable as possible for both of you and the rest of the family, I'm talking about expressing opinions and feelings about your respective responsibilities and lifestyles. These are some fundamental guidelines for feedback that will prevent the procedure from getting tense:

- You must both consent to offering and accepting feedback; otherwise, it will only lead to conflict. Because you are frequently pointing out a blind spot—a quality your partner is actually ignorant of—and because unwelcome observations can be unpleasant and harmful, it can be a perilous endeavour.

- Agree on how to do it, pick the perfect time, and go for a stroll. This will put you side by side and possibly even in step, making it less confrontational. We frequently travelled to the beach in Cornwall when we were there for meetings and to give updates on our progress. Going outside can help you to become more open to new options and ideas.

- If you want to comment on a specific event, do so as soon as you can after it has occurred. The human mind has a peculiar quality that makes it open to accepting helpful criticism right once, but as time goes on, it begins to rationalize and justify.

- Focus your criticism solely on the problem; avoid bringing up personal matters. For example, instead of saying "I'm sick of you never helping me around the home," say "I'd like you to do more around the house so I can start work sooner in the mornings." Your mother spoiled you rotten, etc., so that's her fault.

- Recognize that communicating effectively requires listening to comprehend rather than waiting for a pause to make your argument. After hearing your partner out, you can make your argument; in fact, if you listen carefully, you might not need to. o Be mindful that communicating effectively involves listening to understand rather than waiting for a pause to make your argument. After hearing your partner out, you can express your argument. If you listen carefully, though, you might find that the real problem is something else entirely, and you won't even need to make that point.

- Always criticize the behaviour, never the individual. Say, "That wasn't a really helpful answer to the situation," as opposed to "Why are you being so bolshie?" Instead of asking yourself, "Why are you continuously putting me down in front of customers?" focus on the impact that behaviour had on you. For example, "When you said that to the customer it made me feel incredibly small."

- Remember once more that this isn't only a procedure for providing unfavourable criticism. Your conversation will flow much more easily if you make a point of highlighting all the thoughtful and helpful things your partner does.

IF YOUR SPOUSE WORKS FROM HOME

The old proverb "I married you for life, but not for lunch" was originally mostly used by wives whose husbands had retired and were cluttering the house during the day, but it might now be a piece of advice for couples who both work from home. Being at home together all day can be a shock if you are accustomed to spending the day apart and getting together for dinner to talk about your day. Here are my recommendations for maintaining a healthy relationship while both partners work from home. My partner has, at various points, worked in an office, been away for the entirety of the workweek, and worked full time at home.

- Have separate offices, preferably away from one another's hearing, so you may each work in your own unique ways without disturbing the other.

- If you're using a computer or other piece of equipment with someone else, decide in advance who will do what and when so that you don't lose time waiting for them to finish.

- Respect your partner's working style, especially if it differs from your own and is especially important if they are engaged in creative work. If you even poke your head around the door and say, "Fancy a coffee?"

they can be in the middle of something and become distracted.

- Don't try to work too "coordinated"; your pace of work might not coincide with theirs. Hence, don't feel bad if you take breaks at various times.

- Spending too much time together might cause a relationship to become stale and stressful. You both will have interests outside the home if you make a point of getting out independently, have separate friends and activities, and have different interests.

IF YOUR PARTNER WORKS FROM HOME AND IS PART OF THE SAME COMPANY

Working together in the same business multiplies what is happening in a relationship many times over, just as working from home tends to exaggerate what is already happening in a relationship. According to Jane, a B&B owner, "Working together can be quite taxing on a marriage, but Peter and I get along wonderfully." Our standards are comparable because we both have a tendency to be a little perfectionist. We only fight when we're exhausted; since you can't yell at the visitors, we yell at each other instead, but we've learned to recognize it.

When things are going well, starting a business with your partner may be satisfying in many ways and strengthen your relationship. If things aren't going well, in addition to the strains on the business and the relationship, you might also be dealing with financial concerns, especially if the business is your only source of income. When starting a business together, you should carefully consider your financial situation since it is a big source of relationship conflict.

- How will the workload be distributed? The optimum situation is when you have complementing skills, for as when she is good at administration and customer service and he is good at going out and getting the job done. In order to make decisions on who will do what, it is helpful to have a solid understanding of your personalities and natural talents. Make a list of every job that needs to be done to manage the company, and then assign each individual the jobs based on what they are best at. Consider getting a personality profile done if you're unsure or if you want to improve underutilized skills. People are astounded by their accuracy, and they aid in locating hidden ability.

- It's critical to comprehend how you feel about taking risks. If one of you is gung-ho and the other is cautious anytime there is a chance to grow or do something different, it could be a serious issue. You will both be happier doing different things if your attitudes toward risk are quite different.

- It's crucial to come to an agreement on how much money should be taken from the business for living expenses as well as how it should be used. Likewise, it will be healthier for your relationship if you earn and spend money separately if your priorities are really different.

- Keep changing your working connection, don't forget. It doesn't have to be that way forever just because she handled all the networking when you first started and you handled the technical stuff. Test out various options to see how they perform. Even so, switching up your routine can help you come up with new ideas and get out of a rut.

- Avoid talking exclusively about business. When you suddenly have a wonderful idea while taking a bath or doing the dishes, it can be difficult to hold onto it. However, try to save it like you would if you were working away from home. I doubt you would call your boss in the middle of the night to share your latest epiphany.

- Keep in mind that you are in a relationship outside of work, and make time to nourish both by taking regular weekends off and evenings out. (Visiting restaurants, hotels, and shopping may give you business ideas, but while you're gone, put your relationship first.) Ideally, you will be able to encourage one another and offer consolation to each other when they are sad.

WHEN YOUR PARTNER DOES NOT WORK

Even if you are hidden behind a closed door, if your partner doesn't work, it could come as a surprise to them to have someone at home all day when they used to have the house to themselves. As modifications are made to the new arrangements, some compromising may be necessary.

WORKING FROM HOME AND CHILDREN

When a person first has children and wants to spend more time with them, a lot of individuals start to consider working from home. In theory, it seems like the best method to balance your personal and professional obligations, but it can be challenging to pull off in practice.

On the other side, a youngster who has a parent who works from home may gain from understanding the relationship between job and money and may even learn how to be an entrepreneur.

But, if you work for yourself and developing a great business must always come first, you could feel that your family life suffers as a result.

WORKING FROM HOME AND HAVING KIDS

Although this naturally reduces the amount of time available to perhaps four or five hours a day at most (without taking into account how exhausted you might be looking after a new baby), fitting work around childcare is easier when they are still babies because you can work around their naps. When you need to focus on your work, little toddlers may clamour for your attention.

Although you'll need to come up with your own strategies for finishing your work and making time for your kids, other people's experiences might be useful.

- You might discover that your loyalties are divided and come to the conclusion that you cannot "have it all."

- Little kids don't comprehend the idea of "Don't bother Daddy; he's working." One of the home schoolers I know secured the door to his office with a lock so that his kids couldn't bother him, but it wouldn't work for many kids.

- Work flexible hours in the mornings while the kids are at day care or school and in the evening after they are in bed.

- Take turns providing childcare with family and friends. Since the cost of child care would significantly reduce Nicki's income, she makes every effort to avoid doing so. However, she plans what she refers to as "favour swaps" with her loved ones. She takes care of her cousin's kids one day a week, and her cousin watches hers for the other, giving them both a day off.

- Depending on your line of work, being honest with your customers may be lot less stressful.

(See Chapter 4 on selecting whether to host meetings at home and Chapter 6 on keeping a professional image if you are unsure how to balance children and work commitments.)

- As Hilary discovered, it might be wise to keep your computer passwords out of your children's reach because they could unwittingly get you into a lot of trouble.

HAVING TEENAGERS AND WORKING FROM HOME

Teenagers can be an unpredictable and rather volatile force in the atmosphere where you are attempting to be professional. Little children may require more of your time, but they are more obedient and simpler to maintain to a regular pattern.

No problem can be solved easily. Your issue is particular to you and requires distinct reactions due to aspects like your personality, the personality of your teenager, your family circumstances, and the location of your workplace in the home. Then, try some of these suggestions.

- Establish limitations on how much time is spent using a phone, the volume of music that is appropriate, when you should be bothered, and so on. Don't be surprised if these boundaries are regularly broken. Set the boundaries consistently.

- Approach your potential accomplishments with as much pragmatism and flexibility as you can. Decide which tasks you can avoid doing and which you absolutely must complete.

- Make the most of the hours they are sleeping in (hopefully till early afternoon), hanging out with friends, and in school or college.

- Recognize that you can't wear both a mother hat and a work hat at once, and look for strategies to reduce the amount of emotion in your interactions.

- To prevent disputes over phone use, install a separate phone line and keep it off-limits.

- Caroline comments, "Doing errands is good." To ensure some peace and quiet for a bit, "send them off to walk the dog or go shopping." By paying them to complete a few tiny tasks, you may also play on their mercenary side.

- If at all feasible, involve them in your business and let others set an example for how to conduct yourself professionally. They may, with any hope, learn future-ready talents.

MANAGING VISITORS IN YOUR HOME

Whether or whether you should hold meetings at home was a topic we covered in Chapter 4. There is no dispute about it for some people who work from home since they live "above the shop" and charge clients and customers to enter their residence. The following three couples also had to figure out how to deal with strangers invading their personal space on top of the challenges of finding a method to operate harmoniously together and switching off while not attending to their clients. This is their personal account of the encounter.

Evening cafes at least shut down and let their patrons go. The proprietors of bed and breakfast lodging don't have that convenience. Try having clients who stay the night and want a prepared breakfast the next morning if you feel like work calls and emails are invading your home!

By living in one terraced house and hosting their guests in the one next door, Jane and Peter have a brilliant solution for retaining their privacy while running a B&B. But, because their house is wired with a doorbell, a fire alarm, and a bell for visitors, they are never off duty.

9

IF A CRISIS ARISES, WHAT THEN?

The continual presence of co-workers who can provide you with advice, direction, and a sympathetic ear when things aren't going well is a crucial component of the camaraderie of office life. When you work from home, it's harder to access that easy supply of guidance, so you might find yourself needing to handle a variety of situations on your own.

This chapter addresses:

1.   The types of problems that could arise for even the most well-prepared student doing homework, including those involving money, family, technology, other people, bad luck, getting stuck, and running out of time. Added to that is the turmoil that a golden opportunity might cause.

2.   A selection of ideas that you can use to boost your mood and effectively deal
        with any setbacks while maintaining your composure.

WHAT MIGHT POSSIBLY FAIL?

I've occasionally thought that I'm the only one dealing with difficulties. and failures at work, while some seem to cruise through life, winning achievements and plaudits along the way. This sense of solitude is only exacerbated by the propensity of businesspeople to gloss over issues and keep problems to themselves out of fear of being perceived as unsuccessful. Business publications and courses tend to avoid mentioning the likelihood of mistakes in favour of focusing on how to do things correctly. (With the commendable exception of Cheryl Rickman's, The Small Business Start-up Workbook, which is included in the Resources section of Chapter 4 and has interviews with well-known people about their mistakes and what they learned from them.)

It can be tough to think clearly about your issue and come up with innovative solutions if you have the impression that you are somehow more unfortunate than others and special in being cursed with troubles. Everybody deals with issues of varied severity on a regular basis; therefore, it is preferable to view issues as a natural part of life rather than as tragedies that exclusively affect you. The list of potential problems that can occur for any homeworker is provided below in the hopes that by discussing them openly, they will become less serious. Continue reading the next part of proposed solutions after you have completed reading about these potential problems so you can leave feeling upbeat and confident in your ability to handle any challenges that working from home may present.

FINANCIAL CONCERNS

Financial concerns can be the most severe and incapacitating of all because the majority of us depend on our salary to support ourselves and our families. This is true for both employed individuals concerned about keeping their jobs in a challenging economic environment and self-employed individuals competing in a market that is continuously striving to minimize expenses.

Worrying about money might make you feel driven to earn at your present or a greater pace, and driving yourself too hard can affect your performance and actually lower your chances of succeeding at work. They may appear in several forms.

LOSING YOUR JOB OR THE WORK YOU DO ON CONTRACT

More and more individuals are having to adjust to living with this concern, and that's
actually, the best you can hope for. I was always conscious of the fact that there were other competitors in the cleaning business, almost all of whom would be prepared to perform the work for less money than I was charging. On occasion, I would see leaflets on doormats promoting cleaning services and worry that my clients would be persuaded to do business somewhere else. It took me some time, but I gradually came to the realization that there would always be a chance of losing business and that the only thing I could do in a practical sense was to produce my best work, uphold positive relationships with my clients, and hope for the best. That's the only thing any of us can do. Thinking about potential future events just reduces your effectiveness.

NOT SAVING MONEY

Though it's an overused cliche, it's all too true that change is occurring at an accelerated rate. You have to keep your eye on the ball to ensure that your work remains profitable, which is one of the side effects of perpetual change. Numerous industries are reducing costs by outsourcing work, automating manual activities, or working with giant corporations that can compete with smaller businesses due to economies of scale. As a result, the pay you are offered for a job may be lower than it was previously, rather than rising in step with inflation. Realizing that your lucrative niche no longer pays as well is unpleasant.

Failing to secure a job or contract

Your mind gets to work as soon as you decide to apply for a new job or submit a bid for a project, not only preparing your application or bid but also picturing the accolades you'd receive, how getting the job would affect your life, and how your lifestyle would improve as a result of the additional income. That's a significant time, effort, and emotional investment, so it may be devastating if it doesn't work out.

EMERGENCIES INVOLVING FAMILY AND THE HOME

When you work from home, anything that occurs there or to any of your household members has the potential to affect your daily schedule. Before work is done for the day, you can't rush out the door in the morning and ignore your home life. These kinds of events could happen.

DEATHS OR INFECTIONS

The most upsetting difficulties you're probably going to have while working from home are illnesses or accidents. Being available means that you are the one who will likely have to handle them, whether that means rushing a child to the casualty department or pausing your work to prepare beverages and snacks for a family member who is bedridden.

Of course, you could get sick or have an accident, but in these cases, working from home could be advantageous. You may pace yourself to work when you feel like it and take breaks when you get weary while you recuperate rather than struggling to work while feeling awful. (But, as described in Chapter 8, take care to maintain a good balance between your professional obligations and your own fitness.)

EMERGENCIES IN THE HOME

I refer to the annoying and upsetting hiccups that might occur in any family as "domestic crises." On the coldest day of the year, the boiler breaks down, leaving you shivering and angry, or a rainstorm knocks out your power, effectively closing you off from the outside world and making it impossible to work.

HOUSE MOVING

Moving is not an emergency in the sense that it comes on rapidly; on the contrary, it may take months to complete. A house transfer is particularly upsetting for people who work from home because their home serves as both their job and their primary residence.

To keep the home in good condition for potential buyers, there is further cleaning and maintenance to be done. Then, there is packing up, which includes packing up your workstation. It's astonishing how much material, especially heavy items, may spill out of a filing cabinet. Not to mention how much of a disturbance to work the moving day was and how much time it took to go back to normal after arriving at the new location. Friends had told me before our recent move that they had trouble acquiring new phone lines, but it was still a rude shock to have to wait two weeks for the phone and nearly a month for broadband.

IT Glitches

For those who work from home, communication is essential, so breakdowns might disrupt your daily schedule. These days, we are all more or less dependent on technology, and when it fails, it can be challenging to accomplish anything linked to our daily routine.

AS SOON AS THE TECHNOLOGY FAILS

There are many different ways that technology might fail you, and sometimes those failures are utterly beyond your control. In my situation, the annoying string of hiccups and delays in the telecom company's order procedure were to blame.

Margaret experienced a terrifying moment when her computer, which had previously been dependable, experienced a fatal crash and she was in danger of losing hours of work.

WHEN YOUR IT SKILLS EXPIRE

Many of us learned about computers by osmosis—learning as we went along, scrounging random bits of knowledge from colleagues when needed—and generally wishing for the best.

A small detail might cause a frustrating, grinding halt when you need a little more knowledge or run into an unanticipated problem.

Individual Issues

In your field of work, there are certain to be a few people you interact with regularly that have an impact on your productivity. These could be your co-workers at the corporate office, the stationery store that provides your paper, or the individuals who are employed directly by you or under contract. Despite the greatest of intentions on both ends, there is always a chance for miscommunication in every human relationship, and occasionally, people may just let you down.

UNFAVORABLE CIRCUMSTANCES

Some people believe they are lucky, some think they are unlucky, and some don't think there is such a thing as luck at all. An intriguing perspective on the matter is offered by Deepak Chopra, who claims that luck occurs when chance and readiness coincide. According to his concept, little planning or a genuine opportunity would be considered "poor luck."

We all occasionally experience bad luck that seems to come out of nowhere, regardless of how you feel about luck. Things like vehicle accidents, packages going missing in the mail, trains or planes cancelling on the way to an appointment, and other frustrating and puzzling minor anomalies can have a big impact on how things turn out.

GETTING HUNG UP

Regardless of where we work, everyone has obstacles in their work from time to time. Nevertheless, when working from home, you must rely on your own inventiveness to find solutions or new sources of inspiration. It's important to figure out why you're exhausted before you can accomplish that. Is it that you need a break, you don't have the necessary knowledge, or you have been doing the same thing for too long?

TIME IS OF THE ESSENCE

The knowledge that you may have to deliver a project late due to running out of time is one of the most unpleasant thoughts. Perhaps you didn't give yourself enough time to begin with or you allowed other things to divert your attention and time.

A WONDERFUL CHANCE

It's vital to keep in mind that not all crises are unpleasant as we wrap up this part. For instance, you might receive a call out of the blue offering you a ton of work, which you want to accept but will result in a lot of disruption.

You could need to rearrange your present workload and clients, persuade your family of the advantages of the new position and encourage them to assist you with household chores, arrange travel and accommodations, communicate with others, or hire employees. Making the decision to take advantage of such chances is both thrilling and terrifying since it requires you to step outside of your comfort zone and assume new responsibilities.

HOW TO STAY CALM DURING TIMES OF CRISIS

This section focuses on overcoming any cold sweats you may have as quickly as possible. Overcoming hurdles improves your ability to be creative and overcome challenges in the future. In actuality, people are paid to solve difficulties, and the bigger the problem you can resolve, the more probable it is that you will receive a payment. Here is some advice on how to make the most of the circumstance, get back up, and go on—hopefully wiser and more resourceful than before.

REMOVE YOURSELF FROM THE ISSUE.

My preferred method of solving any problem is to run away from it, as long as you don't use this as an excuse to put off getting started. Avoid continuing to smash your head against that obstacle by leaving and seeking excitement elsewhere. If you just give your conscious mind a break, you'll be shocked at how concepts and answers will appear out of thin air.

BELIEVE IN YOUR INSTINCTS

When you don't feel like working, don't make yourself. We have been heavily conditioned to believe that every minute must be used for something constructive, which typically involves work-related activities. Working from home offers significant independence, so practice listening to your intuition about what to do at any given moment. It might be difficult to overcome the habit of feeling bad if you don't work all day. I have frequently put off doing a certain task while wondering why, just to have it become simpler to finish after finding a crucial piece of knowledge.

ACT IN A DIFFERENT WAY

Regardless of how odd or ordinary, do something utterly unusual. My imagination tends to run wild when I clean the bathroom. The brain cells start firing as soon as I put on the rubber gloves and take the cream cleaner in my hand; a few minutes earlier, I might have been sitting there staring blankly at the computer screen without an idea in my head. However, once I do, I have to stop and jot down all the ideas that come to me. Former London coach Veronica discovered that her best ideas were almost always generated in Starbucks.

CHANGE THE LOCATION OF YOUR WORK

No matter how pleasant and effective your workstation is, it might occasionally become monotonous. In certain situations, a change of scenery can be beneficial. Sit by a window with a new perspective or move to the kitchen table. Take your work outside if it's nice out.

Find out whether your neighbourhood library provides free wi-fi or internet access if what you're missing is people and living. Although all except the larger chains tend to charge, wi-fi is available at cafés in even tiny communities. For other alternatives to working from home, see Chapter 4.

REST ON IT

a tried-and-true approach that works well for all kinds of problems. Also, it's the ideal pretext for an afternoon nap (see Chapter 5).

RETAIN THE DAY

Once more, this entails defying expectations and having faith that something positive will result. I always find that spending the day in a new setting—whether it be going for a stroll in the countryside, browsing art galleries, or having lunch with friends—gives me a rush of extra energy and makes me return to my desk feeling energized and upbeat rather than exhausted and nervous.

When we're struggling and nothing seems to be working, we've often discovered that if we leave the situation for the day and forget about it, we'll get a call or email regarding work. Being able to unwind tends to advance things.

SET OUT TO NETWORK

Meeting new people will give you energy, and you might even learn something important. For further information on how to maximize networking opportunities, see Chapter 7.

WORK OUT THE BLUES

Susan attends three gym sessions each week as a chance to get out of the house and work off her frustrations now that she works from home. A good approach to distinguish between work and leisure time is through exercise (see Chapters 5 and 8 for more ideas).

ENJOY YOUR HOLIDAY

There is no requirement that it take place abroad or even in a remote location. A city break is ideal if you live in the country and vice versa since the most important thing is that you experience a different atmosphere. Even when you remain in the same culture, moving to a new location somehow opens your eyes to other ways of being and doing things. It can spark creative inspiration and help you move past complete blocks.

Plan Ahead

Sometimes circumstances erupt out of the blue and knock us for a loop, but frequently it's possible to anticipate a potential issue and have a plan prepared to minimize it.

the disturbance. Do your own risk assessment on the likelihood that an emergency will occur and several strategies to cope if it does. If you thought it through when your life is running well, you can quickly put your plan into action when everything is flipped upside down.

PLANS FOR IT CONTINGENCIES

An excellent illustration of this kind of contingency planning is anything involving office technology. Consider as many viable solutions as you can, which may include the following, as office equipment often malfunctions when it is most needed.

- Build a positive working relationship with a computer engineer.
- Do routine computer maintenance to speed up the speed at which the programs run.
- Secure your PC against malware and hackers.
- Keep your home computer and work computer separate, especially if you have kids. Free software has a risk of crashing and introducing problems.
- Every night, get your data backed up off-site.
- Request occasional assistance from a family member who is knowledgeable in Technology. Purchase a broadband dongle.
- Look up places in your neighbourhood that provide free internet connection, such as coffee shops, libraries, work hubs (see Chapter 4), or a neighbour's wireless network.
- Maintain plenty supplies of paper and ink, as well as a spare keyboard (which you can purchase for less than £10).

- Bring your phone charger with you to ensure that you never run out of juice.

PLANS FOR PEOPLE IN CRISIS

Mishaps involving technology are generally straightforward to plan for, but those involving people are frequently a little more. Consider what you would do if your child became ill. Would someone be available to take care of them if you had appointments to keep, or would you need to cancel? In an emergency, setting up a "favour swaps" arrangement now will be beneficial; Chapter 8 discusses how to work from home while taking care of kids.

GET SOME EXPERIENCE READY

If you have someone you can rely on already in place, dealing with a setback is easier. support. You might be able to get advice from your supervisor or co-workers, or you could hunt for a professional.

Mentors

A mentor is a person you like and trust who has already travelled the path you are now and who can support you by offering you access to their network in addition to words of encouragement. Big organizations frequently offer formal mentorship programs. You can also ask a respected person to meet you for lunch on a regular basis. As long as they are upfront about how much time they will need to communicate, people are typically flattered to be asked and happy to assist.

Coaches

A coach is more likely to support you in achieving a specific objective over a shorter amount of time than a mentor would, such as getting a promotion or stepping up your business. When the going gets difficult, working with someone who knows the appropriate questions to ask will help you accomplish more than you could on your own. The chapter 3 section on important persons to know when starting a business may also be of interest to you.

Courses

If you have a job, your employer most likely informs you about the most recent skills needed to perform your duties effectively. It's crucial for self-employed people to avoid becoming so obstructively focused on the task at hand that they fall behind. Although taking training courses can appear time-consuming and excessively expensive, they frequently have numerous unanticipated advantages in terms of boosting your confidence and sparking ideas. Many fields offer free or heavily discounted training; for further information, see the Resources section at the conclusion of the chapter.

Casual Assistance

It's not necessary for knowledge and proficiency to be acquired through a formal training program or to be expensive. The teenager you or someone else knows might be the perfect person to ask for Technology advice.

Meeting with a friend in the same profession on a regular basis can be a lifesaver for continued moral support and an opportunity to get out of the house. A sympathetic ear and the opportunity to share worries can make the difference between feeling overwhelmed and maintaining optimism, just as professional counsellors are required to regularly see a supervisor who listens to their concerns about clients and offers advice on how to handle challenging cases. I don't think this book would have been written, much less obtained a publisher, without our weekly chats with a fellow author who was experiencing the same uncertainties and problems.

Put It in Perspective

What just happened probably feels like a complete catastrophe right now, but will it still seem that way in ten years, two years, or even next month? In fact, a few years from now, you'll likely have forgotten about the majority of your "disasters." You'll experience less stress if you think long term.

Alternatively, taking a step back and putting the incident in the perspective of your job and your entire life may be helpful. Sue remembers that by working from home, she is saving herself two hours a day in commute time, which helps her put her concerns about her dependence on the internet into perspective.

Make good use of a downtime moment.

Your ability to complete your work may be hindered because your electricity failed during a storm, your phone line was disconnected, or your computer crashed. Being cut off from the internet is a strangely disorienting experience, but there must be something you can do to pass the time until normal service is restored.

What about the paperwork you keep meaning to file but never do? the individuals you've been meaning to call? The workplace redesigns you've been dying to undertake, but haven't had the time to? You might find that taking a break from routine work allows you to upgrade your workplace and organizational methods, making you more productive once you resume work.

There may be moments when you work for yourself when no one returns your calls or emails, when agreements are breached, and you feel like a leper of the twenty-first century corporate world. Use the time to network or organize your filing cabinet if, for some reason, the voracious jaws of commerce have temporarily spat you out. Soon everyone will have you back at their beck and call.

Choose Your Answer.

If you have a strong emotional attachment to a certain topic or are prone to becoming side-tracked by little setbacks, it is beneficial to learn how to respond to situations in a more optimistic manner than you are accustomed to. Any event can be seen from a variety of angles, as you may have discovered while asking a friend for compassion after going through a trying situation only to find that they didn't share your perspective.

Thinking back to past instances that at first seemed awful and how things ultimately went out is a fantastic method to establish the habit. You might have lost your work and thought your life was over, but you later discovered a position that fitted you far better and offered higher chances. The day after receiving your notice, you were in despair.

Nevertheless, a few weeks or months later, you were relieved that it had happened since, without that push, you might not have looked for another employment. You just need to get to that good feeling a little bit faster. It's possible that a far more brilliant and approachable employee will take the place of the staff member who abruptly upped and departed. If you don't get that contract, perhaps you'll be free to take on something else the following week that opens up a completely new field.

Don't enquire as to why, but do request feedback

There is little value in trying to figure out why something has happened or why it happened to you. You are wasting your time and energy by dwelling on a question that will never have a suitable resolution. Nonetheless, it might be beneficial to get some input from the people involved, including the reason the contract was given to someone else. In order to increase your chances, the following time, you must be ready for an honest response when you ask for this kind of criticism. It won't help you if you see it as a personal slight or a sign that you aren't good enough.

Moreover, keep in mind that the decision-maker might have moved on to other tasks and be too busy to offer the kind of comments you would find most helpful. If getting no response would be even more upsetting than asking, it would be best to assume that they are reluctant to change their mind.

You "can't win them all,"

the kind of statement that, while it may irritate you, is accurate. It is certain that you will occasionally fail, regardless of how diligently you work or how well you prepare. Even if direct mail campaigns have a success rate of as little as 2%, marketing firms continue to distribute their promotional materials because a sizable part of them don't result in any sales. Simply put, they evaluate their odds of success and make plans appropriately.

Failures Happen to Even the Most Successful Persons

The media often gives us the impression that some people have a special touch and are successful in all they undertake. From there, it's only a little step to concluding that we lack the "golden touch" and will never succeed if we have failed at something.

Yet, according to Business Link, 50% of new businesses fail during the first three years, and 20% fail within the first year of operation. As a result, it makes sense that even extraordinarily successful people running a number of enterprises have failed; in fact, they must have experienced more failures than the rest of us in order to attain their achievements. You'll learn how many challenges and problems your own heroes—the ones you think have accomplished amazing things—had to endure in order to succeed if you read the biographies and autobiographies of them.

Failure Does Not Exist; Feedback Does

Depending on the situation, you may have found this remark to be consoling or infuriating when you first heard it. Since we learn at a young age that success is good and failure is bad, many individuals are reluctant to take the risk of attempting anything new in case they fail. It is much better to see life in terms of growth and learning; if something will help you learn something, then it is worth attempting, even if you ostensibly "fail."

Share Your Pain

You realize the significance of having a network of people you can call for a good old moan and a reassuring dose of sympathy when you're in the midst of a crisis. Just be careful not to constantly dump on the same poor person or to just contact when there is an issue, and read Chapter 7 for further information on how to create a strong network of allies.

The first year of Susan's business was challenging, but the pain was lessened by being able to speak with others who had experienced the same thing. "My partner is self-employed and understands how challenging it is when you start a business, so he was incredibly helpful," she said. In addition, I talked to others who had experienced similar things, who reassured me that my circumstance was not at all unique and that I should give it time.

Simply Move Forward.

The title of this section is credited to Annie, who works from home handling payroll and bookkeeping, is preparing for her accountancy exams, has a baby, a ten-year-old, and a husband who is gone all day at work. Annie also has a new born and a ten-year-old. When questioned about how she manages to juggle all of the competing demands on her time and energy, Annie simply responded, "Well, you just carry on, don't you? Many other homeworkers I spoke to shortly after her response repeated it.

I was surprised by Annie's unflappability, but at first, I thought her response was a little mundane and unhelpful because I was waiting for a secret formula for success.

impart. Yet after a while, I understood that the best counsel for a homeworker is to "simply get on with it." You're probably better off continuing with your office work if you're not willing to merely keep going in the face of difficulties and disappointments.

It's also true that the only way to learn how to do anything properly is to... just do it. Although it won't result in any action, theorizing is OK. Beginning is the hardest part; you may modify and fine-tune later.

Recognize the Situation

After the first shock and disappointment has worn off, try to think as rationally as you can be able to explain why you failed. Was it a result of anything you failed to do, something involving a change in policy or a decision-maker that was beyond your control, or just poor luck?

If you've reached a dead end with a project and are unable to make it work, you may have somehow gotten off course. Take a deep breath, stand back, and stop stressing about it. Then, consider your goals.

There may be an emotional issue going on that is unrelated to your professional life if you just can't seem to get started on a project and you can't figure out why; if there seems to be more of a barrier than mere procrastination. Chatting to someone close to you could help you find the underlying feeling and get moving again.

Laughing is Necessary.

And last, but by no means least, it's true that you sometimes have to laugh because you would otherwise cry. No matter how dire a situation initially looks to be, there's always has to be a humorous side somewhere, and learning to recognize it will be very helpful. You can chuckle at the absurdity of the circumstance, other people's quirks, but most of all at yourself. Laughing relieves stress from both the circumstance and yourself, putting you in a better position to decide what to do next and move on. In even the most hopeless circumstances, I can count on a friend to come up with a quirky remark. His humour has helped me feel better countless times.

AFTERWORD

The benefit of working from home is that you don't have to present yourself in a certain way, as if you are still working at an office. The dog can sit at your feet while you sleep during the day or you can take a break from work to do some weeding.

Knowing yourself and what your body and brain require once they are liberated from the confines of a nine-to-five job is the key to making it work. You are in charge.
You may not enjoy some aspects of homeworking, but you are free to adjust anything to suit your preferences and the situation.

You might find the advice I've given to be helpful, but I don't think there are any laws or sophisticated calculations that can guarantee the success of a work-from-home business. Take note of my recommendations and the solutions developed by the individuals profiled here, but don't be afraid to reject them if they don't work for you and look for alternatives.

Working from home can be isolating, so I hope that reading this book will make other homemakers feel relieved to know that they're not the only ones who experience such feelings. Perhaps I'm not crazy after all. You might also like to visit my website, www.workfromhomewisdom.com, if you enjoyed the book.

Good luck on your adventure of working from home; even though the end point may not exist, I hope you find the route to be beneficial.